Java Interview Cracker

Anshuman Mishra

Published by Anshuman Mishra, 2025.

BOOK TITLE: JAVA INTERVIEW CRACKER

OVERVIEW: "JAVA INTERVIEW CRACKER" IS A COMPREHENSIVE GUIDE TAILORED FOR ASPIRING SOFTWARE DEVELOPERS, ESPECIALLY THOSE PREPARING FOR JAVA CODING INTERVIEWS. THIS BOOK IS DESIGNED NOT ONLY FOR STUDENTS ATTENDING COLLEGE BUT ALSO FOR THOSE WHO ARE SERIOUS ABOUT CRACKING INTERVIEWS AND LANDING THEIR DREAM JOBS IN THE TECH INDUSTRY.

CONTENTS:

1. **CHAPTER 1: INTERVIEW-SPECIFIC CHALLENGES**
   - THIS CHAPTER DIVES DEEP INTO THE UNIQUE CHALLENGES CANDIDATES FACE DURING TECHNICAL INTERVIEWS. IT EMPHASIZES UNDERSTANDING COMMON QUESTION PATTERNS USED BY EMPLOYERS AND PROVIDES STRATEGIES ON HOW TO TACKLE THEM EFFECTIVELY. REAL-WORLD EXAMPLES HIGHLIGHT THE IMPORTANCE OF PROBLEM-SOLVING SKILLS AND TECHNICAL KNOWLEDGE.
2. **CHAPTER 2: MOCK INTERVIEW PROBLEMS WITH SOLUTIONS**
   - HERE, READERS WILL FIND A VARIETY OF MOCK INTERVIEW PROBLEMS THAT SIMULATE REAL INTERVIEW SCENARIOS. EACH PROBLEM IS PRESENTED WITH A DETAILED SOLUTION THAT GUIDES CANDIDATES THROUGH THE THOUGHT PROCESS NEEDED TO SOLVE SIMILAR QUESTIONS IN AN ACTUAL INTERVIEW SETTING. THIS HANDS-ON APPROACH PREPARES STUDENTS TO THINK CRITICALLY AND CODE EFFICIENTLY UNDER PRESSURE.
3. **CHAPTER 3: JAVA CODING TEST PREPARATION**
   - THIS CHAPTER FOCUSES ON PREPARING STUDENTS FOR CODING ASSESSMENTS, WHICH ARE COMMON IN TECHNICAL INTERVIEWS. IT INCLUDES A RANGE OF CODING EXERCISES, INCLUDING DATA STRUCTURES, ALGORITHMS, AND JAVA-SPECIFIC CONCEPTS. THE CHAPTER ENCOURAGES PRACTICE AND MASTERY THROUGH REPETITION AND DIVERSE EXAMPLES.
4. **CHAPTER 4: BEST PRACTICES AND TIPS FOR SUCCESS**
   - OFFERING A COLLECTION OF BEST PRACTICES, THIS CHAPTER AIDS STUDENTS IN REFINING THEIR CODING STYLE, DEBUGGING TECHNIQUES, AND INTERVIEW STRATEGIES. ESSENTIAL TIPS ON COMMUNICATION, TIME MANAGEMENT, AND FOLLOW-UP STRATEGIES POST-INTERVIEW ARE ALSO DISCUSSED TO ENSURE A WELL-ROUNDED PREPARATION.

HOW TO STUDY THE BOOK:

- **STRUCTURED LEARNING:** FOLLOW THE CHAPTERS SEQUENTIALLY TO BUILD A SOLID FOUNDATION. START WITH THE INTERVIEW-SPECIFIC CHALLENGES TO UNDERSTAND WHAT IS EXPECTED DURING INTERVIEWS.
- **PRACTICE REGULARLY:** DEDICATE TIME TO WORK THROUGH THE MOCK INTERVIEW PROBLEMS IN CHAPTER 2. TRY TO SOLVE THE PROBLEMS WITHOUT LOOKING AT THE SOLUTIONS FIRST TO MIMIC REAL INTERVIEW CONDITIONS.

- **HANDS-ON CODING:** ACTIVELY CODE THE EXAMPLES PROVIDED THROUGHOUT THE BOOK. SET UP A JAVA DEVELOPMENT ENVIRONMENT AND WRITE OUT THE CODE. THIS PRACTICAL APPLICATION IS CRUCIAL FOR RETAINING CONCEPTS.
- **REVIEW AND REFLECT:** AFTER COMPLETING EACH CHAPTER, TAKE TIME TO REVIEW WHAT YOU'VE LEARNED. SUMMARIZING KEY POINTS CAN HELP REINFORCE YOUR UNDERSTANDING.
- **JOIN STUDY GROUPS:** CONNECT WITH PEERS OR JOIN STUDY GROUPS FOR DISCUSSIONS. TEACHING CONCEPTS TO OTHERS OFTEN REINFORCES YOUR OWN UNDERSTANDING.
- **SIMULATE MOCK INTERVIEWS:** PAIR UP WITH A FRIEND OR MENTOR TO CONDUCT MOCK INTERVIEWS. THIS ENHANCES YOUR SPEAKING AND CODING SKILLS UNDER PRESSURE.

BY FOLLOWING THIS STRUCTURED APPROACH, YOU CAN MAXIMIZE THE EFFECTIVENESS OF "JAVA INTERVIEW CRACKER" IN PREPARING FOR CODING INTERVIEWS AND BUILDING A STRONG FOUNDATION IN JAVA PROGRAMMING.

ABOUT THE AUTHOR:

ANSHUMAN KUMAR MISHRA IS A SEASONED EDUCATOR AND PROLIFIC AUTHOR WITH OVER 20 YEARS OF EXPERIENCE IN THE TEACHING FIELD. HE HAS A DEEP PASSION FOR TECHNOLOGY AND A STRONG COMMITMENT TO MAKING COMPLEX CONCEPTS ACCESSIBLE TO STUDENTS AT ALL LEVELS. WITH AN M.TECH IN COMPUTER SCIENCE FROM BIT MESRA, HE BRINGS BOTH ACADEMIC EXPERTISE AND PRACTICAL EXPERIENCE TO HIS WORK.

CURRENTLY SERVING AS AN ASSISTANT PROFESSOR AT DORANDA COLLEGE, ANSHUMAN HAS BEEN A GUIDING FORCE FOR MANY ASPIRING COMPUTER SCIENTISTS AND ENGINEERS, NURTURING THEIR SKILLS IN VARIOUS PROGRAMMING LANGUAGES AND TECHNOLOGIES. HIS TEACHING STYLE IS FOCUSED ON CLARITY, HANDS-ON LEARNING, AND MAKING STUDENTS COMFORTABLE WITH BOTH THEORETICAL AND PRACTICAL ASPECTS OF COMPUTER SCIENCE.

THROUGHOUT HIS CAREER, ANSHUMAN KUMAR MISHRA HAS AUTHORED OVER 25 BOOKS ON A WIDE RANGE OF TOPICS INCLUDING PYTHON, JAVA, C, C++, DATA SCIENCE, ARTIFICIAL INTELLIGENCE, SQL, .NET, WEB PROGRAMMING, DATA STRUCTURES, AND MORE. HIS BOOKS HAVE BEEN WELL-RECEIVED BY STUDENTS, PROFESSIONALS, AND INSTITUTIONS ALIKE FOR THEIR STRAIGHTFORWARD EXPLANATIONS, PRACTICAL EXERCISES, AND DEEP INSIGHTS INTO THE SUBJECTS.

ANSHUMAN'S APPROACH TO TEACHING AND WRITING IS ROOTED IN HIS BELIEF THAT LEARNING SHOULD BE ENGAGING, INTUITIVE, AND HIGHLY APPLICABLE TO REAL-WORLD SCENARIOS. HIS EXPERIENCE IN BOTH ACADEMIA AND INDUSTRY HAS GIVEN HIM A UNIQUE PERSPECTIVE ON HOW TO BEST PREPARE STUDENTS FOR THE EVOLVING WORLD OF TECHNOLOGY.

IN HIS BOOKS, ANSHUMAN AIMS NOT ONLY TO IMPART KNOWLEDGE BUT ALSO TO INSPIRE A LIFELONG LOVE FOR LEARNING AND EXPLORATION IN THE WORLD OF COMPUTER SCIENCE AND PROGRAMMING.

"JAVA Programming code should be written for developers to comprehend, and only incidentally for the compiler to execute."

— **Anshuman Mishra**

KEY FEATURES

- 100+ CODING PROBLEMS WITH SOLUTIONS
- CONCISE EXPLANATIONS OF CRITICAL JAVA CONCEPTS
- TIPS FOR PRESENTING YOUR SKILLS IN INTERVIEWS
- PRACTICAL EXAMPLES AND SCENARIOS FOR HANDS-ON LEARNING

WHETHER YOU'RE STARTING YOUR CAREER OR PREPARING FOR YOUR NEXT BIG OPPORTUNITY, **"JAVA INTEVIEW CRACKER "** WILL BE YOUR TRUSTED COMPANION ON THE JOURNEY TO SUCCESS.

TABLE OF CONTENTS

Table Of Contents

CHAPTER-1

Interview-Specific Challenges: Solving Tricky Java Programming Puzzles and Commonly Asked Problems

This section focuses on advanced programming puzzles and coding challenges often encountered in interviews, with practical examples and solutions. Additionally, tips for writing optimized and clean code are provided.

1. Solving Tricky Java Programming Puzzles

Puzzle 1: FizzBuzz Challenge
Problem: Write a program that prints the numbers from 1 to 100. For multiples of 3, print "Fizz" instead of the number. For multiples of 5, print "Buzz". For numbers that are multiples of both 3 and 5, print "FizzBuzz".

Solution:

```java
public class FizzBuzz {
    public static void main(String[] args) {
        for (int i = 1; i <= 100; i++) {
            if (i % 3 == 0 && i % 5 == 0) {
                System.out.println("FizzBuzz");
            } else if (i % 3 == 0) {
                System.out.println("Fizz");
            } else if (i % 5 == 0) {
                System.out.println("Buzz");
            } else {
                System.out.println(i);
            }
        }
    }
}
```

Output (Partial):

```
1
2
Fizz
4
Buzz
Fizz
7
8
Fizz
Buzz
11
Fizz
13
```

```
14
FizzBuzz
...
```

Puzzle 2: Prime Numbers Between 1 and 100

Problem: Write a program to print all prime numbers between 1 and 100.

Solution:

```java
public class PrimeNumbers {
    public static void main(String[] args) {
        for (int i = 2; i <= 100; i++) {
            if (isPrime(i)) {
                System.out.println(i);
            }
        }
    }

    public static boolean isPrime(int num) {
        for (int j = 2; j <= Math.sqrt(num); j++) {
            if (num % j == 0) {
                return false;
            }
        }
        return true;
    }
}
```

Output (Partial):

```
2
3
5
7
11
...
```

Puzzle 3: Armstrong Numbers

Problem: Write a program to find all Armstrong numbers between 1 and 1000.

Solution:

```java
public class ArmstrongNumbers {
    public static void main(String[] args) {
        for (int i = 1; i <= 1000; i++) {
            if (isArmstrong(i)) {
                System.out.println(i);
            }
```

```
        }
    }

    public static boolean isArmstrong(int num) {
        int original = num, sum = 0;
        while (num > 0) {
            int digit = num % 10;
            sum += digit * digit * digit;
            num /= 10;
        }
        return sum == original;
    }
}
```

Output:

```
1
153
370
371
407
```

Puzzle 4: Palindrome Check

Problem: Write a program to check if a given number is a palindrome.

Solution:

```
public class PalindromeNumber {
    public static void main(String[] args) {
        int num = 121;
        System.out.println("Is " + num + " a palindrome? " +
isPalindrome(num));
    }

    public static boolean isPalindrome(int num) {
        int original = num, reversed = 0;
        while (num > 0) {
            reversed = reversed * 10 + num % 10;
            num /= 10;
        }
        return original == reversed;
    }
}
```

Output:

```
Is 121 a palindrome? true
```

Puzzle 5: Fibonacci Series

Problem: Write a program to print the first 10 Fibonacci numbers.

Solution:

```
public class FibonacciSeries {
    public static void main(String[] args) {
        int n1 = 0, n2 = 1;
        System.out.print(n1 + " " + n2 + " ");
        for (int i = 2; i < 10; i++) {
            int n3 = n1 + n2;
            System.out.print(n3 + " ");
            n1 = n2;
            n2 = n3;
        }
    }
}
```

Output:

```
0 1 1 2 3 5 8 13 21 34
```

Puzzle 6: Find Factorial

Problem: Write a program to calculate the factorial of a given number.

Solution:

```
public class Factorial {
    public static void main(String[] args) {
        int num = 5;
        System.out.println("Factorial of " + num + " is: " + factorial(num));
    }

    public static int factorial(int num) {
        if (num == 0 || num == 1) return 1;
        return num * factorial(num - 1);
    }
}
```

Output:

```
Factorial of 5 is: 120
```

Puzzle 7: Find Missing Number in an Array

Problem: Given an array of size `n-1` containing numbers from 1 to `n`, find the missing number.

Solution:

```java
public class MissingNumber {
    public static void main(String[] args) {
        int[] nums = {1, 2, 4, 5, 6};
        System.out.println("Missing number: " + findMissingNumber(nums, 6));
    }

    public static int findMissingNumber(int[] nums, int n) {
        int total = n * (n + 1) / 2;
        int sum = 0;
        for (int num : nums) {
            sum += num;
        }
        return total - sum;
    }
}
```

Output:

```
Missing number: 3
```

Puzzle 8: Find Second Largest Element

Problem: Write a program to find the second largest element in an array.

Solution:

```java
public class SecondLargest {
    public static void main(String[] args) {
        int[] nums = {3, 5, 7, 2, 8};
        System.out.println("Second largest element: " +
findSecondLargest(nums));
    }

    public static int findSecondLargest(int[] nums) {
        int largest = Integer.MIN_VALUE, secondLargest = Integer.MIN_VALUE;
        for (int num : nums) {
            if (num > largest) {
                secondLargest = largest;
                largest = num;
            } else if (num > secondLargest && num != largest) {
                secondLargest = num;
            }
        }
```

```
        return secondLargest;
    }
}
```

Output:

```
Second largest element: 7
```

Puzzle 9: Count Occurrences of a Character

Problem: Write a program to count the number of times a specific character appears in a string.

Solution:

```
public class CountCharacter {
    public static void main(String[] args) {
        String str = "Java programming";
        char target = 'a';
        System.out.println("Count of '" + target + "': " +
countOccurrences(str, target));
    }

    public static int countOccurrences(String str, char target) {
        int count = 0;
        for (char c : str.toCharArray()) {
            if (c == target) {
                count++;
            }
        }
        return count;
    }
}
```

Output:

```
Count of 'a': 3
```

Puzzle 10: Check if Two Strings are Anagrams

Problem: Write a program to check if two strings are anagrams.

Solution:

```
import java.util.Arrays;

public class AnagramCheck {
    public static void main(String[] args) {
        String str1 = "listen";
        String str2 = "silent";
```

```
        System.out.println("Are the strings anagrams? " + areAnagrams(str1,
str2));
    }

    public static boolean areAnagrams(String s1, String s2) {
        if (s1.length() != s2.length()) return false;
        char[] arr1 = s1.toCharArray();
        char[] arr2 = s2.toCharArray();
        Arrays.sort(arr1);
        Arrays.sort(arr2);
        return Arrays.equals(arr1, arr2);
    }
}
```

Output:

```
Are the strings anagrams? true
```

Interview Insight:

- **Question:** How can this program be optimized to reduce redundant conditions?
  Answer: Use `StringBuilder` to build the output in one pass.

Puzzle 11: Reverse a String

Problem: Write a program to reverse a string without using any built-in reverse functions.

Solution:

```
public class ReverseString {
    public static void main(String[] args) {
        String str = "JavaProgramming";
        System.out.println("Reversed string: " + reverse(str));
    }

    public static String reverse(String str) {
        String reversed = "";
        for (int i = str.length() - 1; i >= 0; i--) {
            reversed += str.charAt(i);
        }
        return reversed;
    }
}
```

Output:

```
Reversed string: gnimmargorPavaJ
```

Puzzle 12: Count Vowels and Consonants

Problem: Write a program to count the number of vowels and consonants in a given string.

Solution:

```java
public class VowelConsonantCount {
    public static void main(String[] args) {
        String str = "Java Programming";
        int[] result = countVowelsConsonants(str);
        System.out.println("Vowels: " + result[0]);
        System.out.println("Consonants: " + result[1]);
    }

    public static int[] countVowelsConsonants(String str) {
        int vowels = 0, consonants = 0;
        str = str.toLowerCase();
        for (int i = 0; i < str.length(); i++) {
            char c = str.charAt(i);
            if (c == 'a' || c == 'e' || c == 'i' || c == 'o' || c == 'u') {
                vowels++;
            } else if (c >= 'a' && c <= 'z') {
                consonants++;
            }
        }
        return new int[] {vowels, consonants};
    }
}
```

Output:

```
Vowels: 4
Consonants: 10
```

Puzzle 13: Find GCD of Two Numbers

Problem: Write a program to find the greatest common divisor (GCD) of two numbers.

Solution:

```java
public class GCD {
    public static void main(String[] args) {
        int num1 = 56, num2 = 98;
        System.out.println("GCD of " + num1 + " and " + num2 + " is: " +
findGCD(num1, num2));
    }

    public static int findGCD(int num1, int num2) {
        if (num2 == 0) {
```

```
            return num1;
        }
        return findGCD(num2, num1 % num2);
    }
}
```

Output:

```
GCD of 56 and 98 is: 14
```

Puzzle 14: Sum of Digits of a Number

Problem: Write a program to find the sum of digits of a given number.

Solution:

```
public class SumOfDigits {
    public static void main(String[] args) {
        int num = 12345;
        System.out.println("Sum of digits of " + num + " is: " +
sumOfDigits(num));
    }

    public static int sumOfDigits(int num) {
        int sum = 0;
        while (num > 0) {
            sum += num % 10;
            num /= 10;
        }
        return sum;
    }
}
```

Output:

```
Sum of digits of 12345 is: 15
```

Puzzle 15: Merge Two Sorted Arrays

Problem: Write a program to merge two sorted arrays into a single sorted array.

Solution:

```
public class MergeSortedArrays {
    public static void main(String[] args) {
        int[] arr1 = {1, 3, 5, 7};
        int[] arr2 = {2, 4, 6, 8};
```

```java
        int[] merged = mergeArrays(arr1, arr2);
        System.out.println("Merged array: ");
        for (int num : merged) {
            System.out.print(num + " ");
        }
    }

    public static int[] mergeArrays(int[] arr1, int[] arr2) {
        int[] result = new int[arr1.length + arr2.length];
        int i = 0, j = 0, k = 0;
        while (i < arr1.length && j < arr2.length) {
            if (arr1[i] < arr2[j]) {
                result[k++] = arr1[i++];
            } else {
                result[k++] = arr2[j++];
            }
        }
        while (i < arr1.length) {
            result[k++] = arr1[i++];
        }
        while (j < arr2.length) {
            result[k++] = arr2[j++];
        }
        return result;
    }
}
```

Output:

```
Merged array: 1 2 3 4 5 6 7 8
```

Puzzle 16: Check for Anagram of a String

Problem: Write a program to check if two strings are anagrams.

Solution:

```java
import java.util.Arrays;

public class AnagramCheck {
    public static void main(String[] args) {
        String str1 = "listen";
        String str2 = "silent";
        System.out.println("Are the strings anagrams? " + areAnagrams(str1,
str2));
    }

    public static boolean areAnagrams(String s1, String s2) {
        if (s1.length() != s2.length()) return false;
        char[] arr1 = s1.toCharArray();
        char[] arr2 = s2.toCharArray();
        Arrays.sort(arr1);
        Arrays.sort(arr2);
```

```
        return Arrays.equals(arr1, arr2);
    }
}
```

Output:

```
Are the strings anagrams? true
```

Puzzle 17: Sum of Elements in Array

Problem: Write a program to find the sum of elements in an array.

Solution:

```
public class SumArrayElements {
    public static void main(String[] args) {
        int[] arr = {1, 2, 3, 4, 5};
        System.out.println("Sum of elements in array: " + sumOfArray(arr));
    }

    public static int sumOfArray(int[] arr) {
        int sum = 0;
        for (int num : arr) {
            sum += num;
        }
        return sum;
    }
}
```

Output:

```
Sum of elements in array: 15
```

Puzzle 18: Reverse an Array

Problem: Write a program to reverse an array in place.

Solution:

```
public class ReverseArray {
    public static void main(String[] args) {
        int[] arr = {1, 2, 3, 4, 5};
        reverseArray(arr);
        System.out.println("Reversed array: ");
        for (int num : arr) {
            System.out.print(num + " ");
        }
    }
```

```java
    public static void reverseArray(int[] arr) {
        int start = 0, end = arr.length - 1;
        while (start < end) {
            int temp = arr[start];
            arr[start] = arr[end];
            arr[end] = temp;
            start++;
            end--;
        }
    }}
```

Output:

```
Reversed array: 5 4 3 2 1
```

Puzzle 19: Find All Divisors of a Number

Problem: Write a program to find all divisors of a number.

Solution:

```java
public class Divisors {
    public static void main(String[] args) {
        int num = 12;
        System.out.println("Divisors of " + num + ":");
        findDivisors(num);
    }

    public static void findDivisors(int num) {
        for (int i = 1; i <= num; i++) {
            if (num % i == 0) {
                System.out.print(i + " ");
            }
        }
    }
}
```

Output:

```
Divisors of 12: 1 2 3 4 6 12
```

Puzzle 20: Count Words in a Sentence

Problem: Write a program to count the number of words in a sentence.

Solution:

```java
public class WordCount {
    public static void main(String[] args) {
```

```
        String sentence = "Java is a powerful programming language.";
        System.out.println("Number of words: " + countWords(sentence));
    }

    public static int countWords(String sentence) {
        String[] words = sentence.split("\\s+");
        return words.length;
    }}
```

Output:

```
Number of words: 5
```

Puzzle 21: Find the First Non-Repeating Character

Problem: Write a program to find the first non-repeating character in a string.

Solution:

```
public class FirstNonRepeating {
    public static void main(String[] args) {
        String str = "swiss";
        System.out.println("First non-repeating character: " +
firstNonRepeating(str));
    }

    public static char firstNonRepeating(String str) {
        for (int i = 0; i < str.length(); i++) {
            if (str.indexOf(str.charAt(i)) == str.lastIndexOf(str.charAt(i)))
{
                return str.charAt(i);
            }
        }
        return '-';  // Return '-' if no non-repeating character found
    }
}
```

Output:

```
First non-repeating character: w
```

Puzzle 22: Generate Multiplication Table

Problem: Write a program to print the multiplication table of a given number.

Solution:

```java
public class MultiplicationTable {
    public static void main(String[] args) {
        int num = 5;
        System.out.println("Multiplication table of " + num + ":");
        for (int i = 1; i <= 10; i++) {
            System.out.println(num + " x " + i + " = " + (num * i));
        }
    }
}
```

Output:

```
Multiplication table of 5:
5 x 1 = 5
5 x 2 = 10
5 x 3 = 15
...
```

Puzzle 23: Remove Duplicates from an Array

Problem: Write a program to remove duplicates from an array.

Solution:

```java
import java.util.Arrays;

public class RemoveDuplicates {
    public static void main(String[] args) {
        int[] arr = {1, 2, 3, 4, 2, 3, 5};
        arr = removeDuplicates(arr);
        System.out.println("Array without duplicates: " +
Arrays.toString(arr));
    }

    public static int[] removeDuplicates(int[] arr) {
        return Arrays.stream(arr).distinct().toArray();
    }
}
```

Output:

```
Array without duplicates: [1, 2, 3, 4, 5]
}
```

Puzzle 24: Find the Second Largest Element in an Array

Problem: Write a program to find the second largest element in an array without sorting the array.

Solution:

```java
public class SecondLargest {
    public static void main(String[] args) {
        int[] arr = {23, 45, 67, 89, 12, 90};
        System.out.println("Second largest element in the array: " +
findSecondLargest(arr));
    }

    public static int findSecondLargest(int[] arr) {
        int largest = Integer.MIN_VALUE;
        int secondLargest = Integer.MIN_VALUE;

        for (int num : arr) {
            if (num > largest) {
                secondLargest = largest;
                largest = num;
            } else if (num > secondLargest && num != largest) {
                secondLargest = num;
            }
        }

        return secondLargest;
    }
}
```

Output:

```
Second largest element in the array: 67
```

Puzzle 25: Reverse a String Without Using Built-in Functions

Problem: Write a program to reverse a given string without using any built-in reverse methods.

Solution:

```java
public class ReverseString {
    public static void main(String[] args) {
        String str = "Hello, World!";
        System.out.println("Reversed string: " + reverseString(str));
    }

    public static String reverseString(String str) {
        char[] chars = str.toCharArray();
        int left = 0, right = chars.length - 1;
        while (left < right) {
```

```
            char temp = chars[left];
            chars[left] = chars[right];
            chars[right] = temp;
            left++;
            right--;
        }
        return new String(chars);
    }
}
```

Output:

```
Reversed string: !dlroW ,olleH
```

Puzzle 26: Divide by Zero Exception

Problem: Write a program that handles a division by zero exception and displays a custom error message.

Solution:

```
public class DivideByZero {
    public static void main(String[] args) {
        int a = 10, b = 0;
        try {
            int result = a / b;
        } catch (ArithmeticException e) {
            System.out.println("Error: Division by zero is not allowed.");
        }
    }
}
```

Output:

```
Error: Division by zero is not allowed.
```

Puzzle 27: Handle Multiple Exceptions

Problem: Write a program that handles multiple exceptions (e.g., ArithmeticException and NullPointerException) in a single try-catch block.

Solution:

```
public class MultipleExceptions {
    public static void main(String[] args) {
        String str = null;
```

```
        int[] arr = {1, 2, 3};

        try {
            int result = 10 / 0;   // ArithmeticException
            System.out.println(str.length());   // NullPointerException
            System.out.println(arr[5]);   // ArrayIndexOutOfBoundsException
        } catch (ArithmeticException | NullPointerException |
ArrayIndexOutOfBoundsException e) {
            System.out.println("Exception: " + e);
        }
    }
}
```

Output:

```
Exception: java.lang.ArithmeticException: / by zero
```

Puzzle 28: Custom Exception for Invalid Age

Problem: Write a custom exception class InvalidAgeException that is thrown if the user enters an invalid age (e.g., negative age).

Solution:

```
class InvalidAgeException extends Exception {
    public InvalidAgeException(String message) {
        super(message);
    }
}

public class CustomExceptionExample {
    public static void main(String[] args) {
        int age = -5;

        try {
            if (age < 0) {
                throw new InvalidAgeException("Age cannot be negative.");
            }
            System.out.println("Age is: " + age);
        } catch (InvalidAgeException e) {
            System.out.println("Error: " + e.getMessage());
        }
    }
}
```

Output:

```
Error: Age cannot be negative.
```

Puzzle 29: Finally Block Execution

Problem: Write a program to demonstrate the use of the `finally` block, where it executes regardless of whether an exception occurred or not.

Solution:

```java
public class FinallyBlockExample {
    public static void main(String[] args) {
        try {
            System.out.println("Inside try block.");
            int result = 10 / 0;  // This will cause ArithmeticException
        } catch (ArithmeticException e) {
            System.out.println("Exception caught: " + e);
        } finally {
            System.out.println("This will always execute, even if an
exception occurs.");
        }   }}
```

Output:

```
Inside try block.
Exception caught: java.lang.ArithmeticException: / by zero
This will always execute, even if an exception occurs.
```

Puzzle 30: Handle Multiple Exceptions in Different Blocks

Problem: Write a program that demonstrates handling multiple exceptions using separate `catch` blocks.

Solution:

```java
public class MultipleCatchBlocks {
    public static void main(String[] args) {
        String str = null;
        int[] arr = {1, 2, 3};

        try {
            int result = 10 / 0;
        } catch (ArithmeticException e) {
            System.out.println("Arithmetic Exception: " + e.getMessage());
        }

        try {
            System.out.println(str.length());
        } catch (NullPointerException e) {
            System.out.println("NullPointer Exception: " + e.getMessage());
        }

        try {
            System.out.println(arr[5]);
```

```
        } catch (ArrayIndexOutOfBoundsException e) {
            System.out.println("ArrayIndexOutOfBounds Exception: " +
e.getMessage());
        }
    }
}
```

Output:

```
Arithmetic Exception: / by zero
NullPointer Exception: Cannot invoke "String.length()" because "str" is null
ArrayIndexOutOfBounds Exception: Index 5 out of bounds for length 3
```

Puzzle 31: Handle FileNotFoundException

Problem: Write a program that tries to read a file that doesn't exist and catches a
FileNotFoundException.

Solution:

```
import java.io.*;

public class FileNotFoundExceptionExample {
    public static void main(String[] args) {
        try {
            FileReader file = new FileReader("non_existing_file.txt");
            BufferedReader fileInput = new BufferedReader(file);
            fileInput.readLine();
            fileInput.close();
        } catch (FileNotFoundException e) {
            System.out.println("File not found: " + e.getMessage());
        } catch (IOException e) {
            System.out.println("Error reading the file: " + e.getMessage());
        }
    }
}
```

Output:

```
File not found: non_existing_file.txt (No such file or directory)
```

Puzzle 32: Throwing an Exception Manually

Problem: Write a program that demonstrates how to throw an exception manually using the `throw` keyword.

Solution:

```java
public class ThrowExceptionExample {
    public static void main(String[] args) {
        int age = 15;

        try {
            if (age < 18) {
                throw new IllegalArgumentException("Age must be 18 or
older.");
            }
            System.out.println("Age is: " + age);
        } catch (IllegalArgumentException e) {
            System.out.println("Exception: " + e.getMessage());
        }
    }
}
```

Output:

```
Exception: Age must be 18 or older.
```

Puzzle 33: Catching Throwable

Problem: Write a program that demonstrates catching `Throwable` to handle errors and exceptions.

Solution:

```java
public class CatchThrowable {
    public static void main(String[] args) {
        try {
            String str = null;
            System.out.println(str.length());  // NullPointerException
        } catch (Throwable e) {
            System.out.println("Caught Throwable: " +
e.getClass().getSimpleName());
        }
    }
}
```

Output:

```
Caught Throwable: NullPointerException
```

Puzzle 34: Nested Try-Catch Blocks

Problem: Write a program that uses nested try-catch blocks. The inner `catch` block should handle a specific exception and the outer `catch` block should handle a general exception.

Solution:

```java
public class NestedTryCatch {
    public static void main(String[] args) {
        try {
            try {
                int result = 10 / 0;  // ArithmeticException
            } catch (ArithmeticException e) {
                System.out.println("Inner catch: ArithmeticException caught");
                throw e;  // Re-throwing the exception
            }
        } catch (Exception e) {
            System.out.println("Outer catch: General Exception caught");
        }
    }
}
```

Output:

```
Inner catch: ArithmeticException caught
Outer catch: General Exception caught
```

Puzzle 35: Custom Exception for Invalid Input

Problem: Write a custom exception class `InvalidInputException` to handle invalid input from a user.

Solution:

```java
class InvalidInputException extends Exception {
    public InvalidInputException(String message) {
        super(message);
    }
}

public class InvalidInputExample {
    public static void main(String[] args) {
        String input = "abc123";

        try {
            if (!input.matches("[0-9]+")) {
                throw new InvalidInputException("Invalid input: Only numbers are allowed.");
            }
            System.out.println("Valid input: " + input);
```

```
        } catch (InvalidInputException e) {
            System.out.println("Error: " + e.getMessage());
        }
    }
}
```

Output:

```
Error: Invalid input: Only numbers are allowed.
```

Puzzle 36: Reverse a String Without Using Built-in Methods

Problem: Write a program to reverse a string without using the built-in `reverse()` method.

Solution:

```
public class ReverseString {
    public static void main(String[] args) {
        String str = "Java Programming";
        String reversed = "";

        for (int i = str.length() - 1; i >= 0; i--) {
            reversed += str.charAt(i);
        }

        System.out.println("Reversed String: " + reversed);
    }
}
```

Output:

```
Reversed String: gnimmargorP avaJ
```

Puzzle 37: Check if Two Strings Are Anagrams

Problem: Write a program to check if two strings are anagrams.

Solution:

```
import java.util.Arrays;

public class AnagramCheck {
    public static void main(String[] args) {
        String str1 = "listen";
        String str2 = "silent";

        char[] arr1 = str1.toCharArray();
        char[] arr2 = str2.toCharArray();

        Arrays.sort(arr1);
```

```
        Arrays.sort(arr2);

        if (Arrays.equals(arr1, arr2)) {
            System.out.println("The strings are anagrams.");
        } else {
            System.out.println("The strings are not anagrams.");
        }
    }
}
```

Output:

```
The strings are anagrams.
```

Puzzle 38: Count the Occurrences of a Character in a String

Problem: Write a program to count the number of occurrences of a specific character in a string.

Solution:

```java
public class CharacterCount {
    public static void main(String[] args) {
        String str = "Java programming is fun!";
        char character = 'a';
        int count = 0;

        for (int i = 0; i < str.length(); i++) {
            if (str.charAt(i) == character) {
                count++;
            }
        }

        System.out.println("The character '" + character + "' occurs " +
count + " times.");
    }
}
```

Output:

```
The character 'a' occurs 3 times.
```

Puzzle 39: Check if a String is a Palindrome

Problem: Write a program to check if a string is a palindrome.

Solution:

```java
public class PalindromeCheck {
    public static void main(String[] args) {
        String str = "madam";
        String reversed = "";

        for (int i = str.length() - 1; i >= 0; i--) {
            reversed += str.charAt(i);
        }

        if (str.equals(reversed)) {
            System.out.println("The string is a palindrome.");
        } else {
            System.out.println("The string is not a palindrome.");
        }
    }
}
```

Output:

```
The string is a palindrome.
```

Puzzle 40: Remove Duplicates from a String

Problem: Write a program to remove duplicate characters from a string.

Solution:

```java
import java.util.HashSet;

public class RemoveDuplicates {
    public static void main(String[] args) {
        String str = "programming";
        HashSet<Character> uniqueChars = new HashSet<>();

        StringBuilder result = new StringBuilder();

        for (int i = 0; i < str.length(); i++) {
            if (!uniqueChars.contains(str.charAt(i))) {
                uniqueChars.add(str.charAt(i));
                result.append(str.charAt(i));
            }
        }

        System.out.println("String without duplicates: " + result);
    }}
```

Output:

```
String without duplicates: progamin
```

Puzzle 41: Convert String to Integer

Problem: Write a program to convert a string to an integer without using `Integer.parseInt()`.

Solution:

```java
public class StringToInteger {
    public static void main(String[] args) {
        String str = "12345";
        int number = 0;

        for (int i = 0; i < str.length(); i++) {
            number = number * 10 + (str.charAt(i) - '0');
        }

        System.out.println("Converted Integer: " + number);
    }
}
```

Output:

```
Converted Integer: 12345
```

Puzzle 42: Find the First Non-Repeating Character

Problem: Write a program to find the first non-repeating character in a string.

Solution:

```java
import java.util.HashMap;

public class FirstNonRepeating {
    public static void main(String[] args) {
        String str = "swiss";
        HashMap<Character, Integer> map = new HashMap<>();

        for (int i = 0; i < str.length(); i++) {
            map.put(str.charAt(i), map.getOrDefault(str.charAt(i), 0) + 1);
        }

        for (int i = 0; i < str.length(); i++) {
            if (map.get(str.charAt(i)) == 1) {
```

```
                System.out.println("First non-repeating character: " +
str.charAt(i));
                break;
            }
        }
    }
}
```

Output:

```
First non-repeating character: w
```

Puzzle 43: Reverse Words in a String

Problem: Write a program to reverse the words in a string, keeping the spaces intact.

Solution:

```
public class ReverseWords {
    public static void main(String[] args) {
        String str = "Java programming is fun";
        String[] words = str.split(" ");
        StringBuilder reversed = new StringBuilder();

        for (int i = words.length - 1; i >= 0; i--) {
            reversed.append(words[i]);
            if (i != 0) {
                reversed.append(" ");
            }
        }

        System.out.println("Reversed String: " + reversed);
    }
}
```

Output:

```
Reversed String: fun is programming Java
```

Puzzle 44: Find the Length of a String Without Using `.length()`

Problem: Write a program to find the length of a string without using the `.length()` method.

Solution:

```
public class StringLength {
    public static void main(String[] args) {
        String str = "Hello, world!";
        int length = 0;
```

```
            try {
                while (true) {
                    str.charAt(length);
                    length++;
                }
            } catch (StringIndexOutOfBoundsException e) {
                System.out.println("Length of the string: " + length);
            }
        }
    }
}
```

Output:

```
Length of the string: 13
```

Puzzle 45: Find the Most Frequent Character

Problem: Write a program to find the most frequent character in a string.

Solution:

```java
import java.util.HashMap;

public class MostFrequentCharacter {
    public static void main(String[] args) {
        String str = "programming";
        HashMap<Character, Integer> map = new HashMap<>();

        for (int i = 0; i < str.length(); i++) {
            map.put(str.charAt(i), map.getOrDefault(str.charAt(i), 0) + 1);
        }

        char maxChar = ' ';
        int maxCount = 0;

        for (char c : map.keySet()) {
            if (map.get(c) > maxCount) {
                maxCount = map.get(c);
                maxChar = c;
            }
        }

        System.out.println("Most frequent character: " + maxChar);
    }
}
```

Output:

```
Most frequent character: r
```

Puzzle 46: Remove Whitespace from a String

Problem: Write a program to remove all whitespaces from a string.

Solution:

```
public class RemoveWhitespace {
    public static void main(String[] args) {
        String str = "  Java programming  is fun  ";
        String result = str.replaceAll("\\s+", "");
        System.out.println("String without whitespaces: " + result);
    }
}
```

Output:

```
String without whitespaces: Javaprogrammingisfun
```

Puzzle 47: Compare Two Strings Ignoring Case

Problem: Write a program to compare two strings ignoring case.

Solution:

```
public class CompareStringsIgnoreCase {
    public static void main(String[] args) {
        String str1 = "java";
        String str2 = "JAVA";

        if (str1.equalsIgnoreCase(str2)) {
            System.out.println("The strings are equal (ignoring case).");
        } else {
            System.out.println("The strings are not equal.");
        }
    }
}
```

Output:

```
The strings are equal (ignoring case).
```

Puzzle 48: Replace All Occurrences of a Character in a String

Problem: Write a program to replace all occurrences of a character in a string with another character.

Solution:

```java
public class ReplaceCharacter {
    public static void main(String[] args) {
        String str = "hello world";
        char oldChar = 'o';
        char newChar = 'a';

        String result = str.replace(oldChar, newChar);
        System.out.println("Updated String: " + result);
    }
}
```

Output:

```
Updated String: hella warld
```

Puzzle 49: Check if a String Contains a Substring

Problem: Write a program to check if a string contains a specific substring.

Solution:

```java
public class ContainsSubstring {
    public static void main(String[] args) {
        String str = "Java programming is fun";
        String substring = "programming";

        if (str.contains(substring)) {
            System.out.println("The string contains the substring.");
        } else {
            System.out.println("The string does not contain the substring.");
        }
    }
}
```

Output:

```
The string contains the substring.
```

Puzzle 50: Concatenate Two Strings

Problem: Write a program to concatenate two strings.

Solution:

```
public class ConcatenateStrings {
    public static void main(String[] args) {
        String str1 = "Hello, ";
        String str2 = "World!";

        String result = str1.concat(str2);
        System.out.println("Concatenated String: " + result);
    }
}
```

Output:

```
Concatenated String: Hello, World!
```

Puzzle 51: Constructor Overloading

Problem: Write a program to demonstrate constructor overloading.

Solution:

```
class Vehicle {
    String type;
    int wheels;

    // Constructor 1
    Vehicle(String type) {
        this.type = type;
        this.wheels = 4;  // Default value
    }

    // Constructor 2
    Vehicle(String type, int wheels) {
        this.type = type;
        this.wheels = wheels;
    }

    void display() {
        System.out.println("Type: " + type + ", Wheels: " + wheels);
    }
}

public class ConstructorOverloading {
    public static void main(String[] args) {
        Vehicle car = new Vehicle("Car");
        Vehicle bike = new Vehicle("Bike", 2);
        car.display();
```

```
        bike.display();
    }
}
```

Output:

```
Type: Car, Wheels: 4
Type: Bike, Wheels: 2
```

Puzzle 52: Constructor Chaining

Problem: Write a program to demonstrate constructor chaining in Java.

Solution:

```
class Animal {
    Animal() {
        System.out.println("Animal is created.");
    }
}

class Dog extends Animal {
    Dog() {
        super();  // Calling the parent class constructor
        System.out.println("Dog is created.");
    }
}

public class ConstructorChaining {
    public static void main(String[] args) {
        Dog dog = new Dog();
    }
}
```

Output:

```
Animal is created.
Dog is created.
```

Puzzle 53: Polymorphism – Method Overloading

Problem: Demonstrate method overloading in Java.

Solution:

```
class MathOperations {
    // Method to add two integers
    int add(int a, int b) {
        return a + b;
```

```
        }

        // Method to add three integers
        int add(int a, int b, int c) {
            return a + b + c;
        }
    }

    public class MethodOverloading {
        public static void main(String[] args) {
            MathOperations math = new MathOperations();
            System.out.println("Sum of 2 numbers: " + math.add(5, 10));
            System.out.println("Sum of 3 numbers: " + math.add(5, 10, 15));
        }
    }
```

Output:

```
Sum of 2 numbers: 15
Sum of 3 numbers: 30
```

Puzzle 54: Polymorphism – Method Overriding

Problem: Demonstrate method overriding in Java.

Solution:

```
class Animal {
    void sound() {
        System.out.println("Animal makes a sound");
    }
}

class Dog extends Animal {
    @Override
    void sound() {
        System.out.println("Dog barks");
    }
}

public class MethodOverriding {
    public static void main(String[] args) {
        Animal animal = new Animal();
        animal.sound();

        Dog dog = new Dog();
        dog.sound();
    }
}
```

Output:

```
Animal makes a sound
Dog barks
```

Puzzle 55: Inheritance – Single Inheritance

Problem: Write a program to demonstrate single inheritance in Java.

Solution:

```java
class Animal {
    void eat() {
        System.out.println("Eating...");
    }
}

class Dog extends Animal {
    void bark() {
        System.out.println("Barking...");
    }
}

public class SingleInheritance {
    public static void main(String[] args) {
        Dog dog = new Dog();
        dog.eat();
        dog.bark();
    }
}
```

Output:

```
Eating...
Barking...
```

Puzzle 56: Inheritance – Multilevel Inheritance

Problem: Write a program to demonstrate multilevel inheritance in Java.

Solution:

```java
class Animal {
    void eat() {
        System.out.println("Eating...");
    }
}
```

```java
class Dog extends Animal {
    void bark() {
        System.out.println("Barking...");
    }
}

class Puppy extends Dog {
    void play() {
        System.out.println("Playing...");
    }
}

public class MultilevelInheritance {
    public static void main(String[] args) {
        Puppy puppy = new Puppy();
        puppy.eat();
        puppy.bark();
        puppy.play();
    }
}
```

Output:

```
Eating...
Barking...
Playing...
```

Puzzle 57: Inheritance – Hierarchical Inheritance

Problem: Demonstrate hierarchical inheritance in Java.

Solution:

```java
class Animal {
    void eat() {
        System.out.println("Eating...");
    }
}

class Dog extends Animal {
    void bark() {
        System.out.println("Barking...");
    }
}

class Cat extends Animal {
    void meow() {
        System.out.println("Meowing...");
    }
}

public class HierarchicalInheritance {
```

```java
    public static void main(String[] args) {
        Dog dog = new Dog();
        dog.eat();
        dog.bark();

        Cat cat = new Cat();
        cat.eat();
        cat.meow();
    }
}
```

Output:

```
Eating...
Barking...
Eating...
Meowing...
```

Puzzle 58: Abstract Class

Problem: Demonstrate the use of an abstract class in Java.

Solution:

```java
abstract class Animal {
    abstract void sound();

    void eat() {
        System.out.println("Eating...");
    }
}

class Dog extends Animal {
    @Override
    void sound() {
        System.out.println("Barking...");
    }
}

public class AbstractClass {
    public static void main(String[] args) {
        Dog dog = new Dog();
        dog.sound();
        dog.eat();
    }
}
```

Output:

```
Barking...
Eating...
```

Puzzle 59: Abstract Method

Problem: Demonstrate an abstract method in an abstract class.

Solution:

```
abstract class Shape {
    abstract void draw();
}

class Circle extends Shape {
    @Override
    void draw() {
        System.out.println("Drawing a Circle");
    }
}

class Square extends Shape {
    @Override
    void draw() {
        System.out.println("Drawing a Square");
    }
}

public class AbstractMethod {
    public static void main(String[] args) {
        Shape shape1 = new Circle();
        shape1.draw();

        Shape shape2 = new Square();
        shape2.draw();
    }
}
```

Output:

```
Drawing a Circle
Drawing a Square
```

Puzzle 60: Method Overriding – Dynamic Method Dispatch

Problem: Demonstrate dynamic method dispatch using method overriding.

Solution:

```
class Animal {
    void sound() {
        System.out.println("Animal makes a sound");
    }
}
```

```java
class Dog extends Animal {
    @Override
    void sound() {
        System.out.println("Dog barks");
    }
}

public class DynamicMethodDispatch {
    public static void main(String[] args) {
        Animal animal = new Dog();
        animal.sound();  // Dynamic method dispatch
    }
}
```

Output:

```
Dog barks
```

Puzzle 61: Constructor in Inheritance

Problem: Demonstrate constructor calling in inheritance.

Solution:

```java
class Animal {
    Animal() {
        System.out.println("Animal is created");
    }
}

class Dog extends Animal {
    Dog() {
        System.out.println("Dog is created");
    }
}

public class ConstructorInheritance {
    public static void main(String[] args) {
        Dog dog = new Dog();
    }
}
```

Output:

```
Animal is created
Dog is created
```

Puzzle 62: Accessing Parent Class Constructor

Problem: Write a program to call a parent class constructor explicitly in a subclass.

Solution:

```java
class Animal {
    Animal() {
        System.out.println("Animal is created");
    }
}

class Dog extends Animal {
    Dog() {
        super();  // Calling parent class constructor
        System.out.println("Dog is created");
    }
}

public class ParentConstructor {
    public static void main(String[] args) {
        Dog dog = new Dog();
    }
}
```

Output:

```
Animal is created
Dog is created
```

Puzzle 63: Static Method in Inheritance

Problem: Write a program to demonstrate static methods in inheritance.

Solution:

```java
class Animal {
    static void eat() {
        System.out.println("Animal is eating");
    }
}

class Dog extends Animal {
    static void eat() {
        System.out.println("Dog is eating");
    }
}

public class StaticMethodInheritance {
    public static void main(String[] args) {
        Animal.eat();
```

```
        Dog.eat();
    }
}
```

Output:

```
Animal is eating
Dog is eating
```

Puzzle 64: Super Keyword

Problem: Demonstrate the usage of the `super` keyword in Java.

Solution:

```
class Animal {
    void eat() {
        System.out.println("Animal is eating");
    }
}

class Dog extends Animal {
    void eat() {
        super.eat();   // Calling parent class method
        System.out.println("Dog is eating");
    }
}

public class SuperKeyword {
    public static void main(String[] args) {
        Dog dog = new Dog();
        dog.eat();
    }
}
```

Output:

```
Animal is eating
Dog is eating
```

Puzzle 65: Method Scope

Problem: Write a program to demonstrate the scope of a method in Java.

Solution:

```
class Example {
    void method1() {
        int x = 5;   // Local variable
```

```
            System.out.println("x in method1: " + x);
    }

    void method2() {
        // System.out.println("x in method2: " + x);   // Error: x is not
accessible here
    }
}

public class MethodScope {
    public static void main(String[] args) {
        Example obj = new Example();
        obj.method1();
        obj.method2();
    }
}
```

Output:

```
x in method1: 5
```

Puzzle 66: Local and Instance Variables

Problem: Demonstrate the scope of local and instance variables.

Solution:

```
class Example {
    int x = 10;   // Instance variable

    void method() {
        int x = 20;   // Local variable
        System.out.println("Local x: " + x);
        System.out.println("Instance x: " + this.x);
    }
}

public class VariablesScope {
    public static void main(String[] args) {
        Example obj = new Example();
        obj.method();
    }}
```

Output:

```
Local x: 20
Instance x: 10
```

Puzzle 67: Connection Creation and Closing

Problem: Demonstrate the creation of a JDBC connection and closing it properly.

```java
import java.sql.*;

public class ConnectionCloseExample {
    public static void main(String[] args) {
        Connection connection = null;
        try {
            connection =
DriverManager.getConnection("jdbc:mysql://localhost:3306/mydb", "root",
"password");
            System.out.println("Connection established.");
        } catch (SQLException e) {
            e.printStackTrace();
        } finally {
            try {
                if (connection != null) {
                    connection.close();
                    System.out.println("Connection closed.");
                }
            } catch (SQLException e) {
                e.printStackTrace();
            }
        }
    }
}
```

Output:

```
Connection established.
Connection closed.
```

Puzzle 68: Statement Execution

Problem: Demonstrate the execution of an UPDATE statement in JDBC.

```java
import java.sql.*;

public class UpdateStatementExample {
    public static void main(String[] args) {
        Connection connection = null;
        Statement statement = null;

        try {
            connection =
DriverManager.getConnection("jdbc:mysql://localhost:3306/mydb", "root",
"password");
            statement = connection.createStatement();
            int rowsAffected = statement.executeUpdate("UPDATE users SET age
= 30 WHERE id = 1");
```

```
            System.out.println(rowsAffected + " row(s) updated.");
        } catch (SQLException e) {
            e.printStackTrace();
        } finally {
            try {
                if (statement != null) statement.close();
                if (connection != null) connection.close();
            } catch (SQLException e) {
                e.printStackTrace();
            }
        }
    }
}
```

Output:

```
1 row(s) updated.
```

Puzzle 69: PreparedStatement with Parameters

Problem: Demonstrate the use of `PreparedStatement` with parameters to prevent SQL injection.

```java
import java.sql.*;

public class PreparedStatementExample {
    public static void main(String[] args) {
        Connection connection = null;
        PreparedStatement preparedStatement = null;

        try {
            connection =
DriverManager.getConnection("jdbc:mysql://localhost:3306/mydb", "root",
"password");
            String sql = "SELECT * FROM users WHERE username = ?";
            preparedStatement = connection.prepareStatement(sql);
            preparedStatement.setString(1, "john_doe");

            ResultSet resultSet = preparedStatement.executeQuery();
            while (resultSet.next()) {
                System.out.println("User: " +
resultSet.getString("username"));
            }
        } catch (SQLException e) {
            e.printStackTrace();
        } finally {
            try {
                if (preparedStatement != null) preparedStatement.close();
                if (connection != null) connection.close();
            } catch (SQLException e) {
                e.printStackTrace();
            }
        }
```

```
        }
}
```

Output:

```
User: john_doe
```

Puzzle 70: Batch Processing

Problem: Demonstrate batch processing with JDBC.

```java
import java.sql.*;

public class BatchProcessingExample {
    public static void main(String[] args) {
        Connection connection = null;
        Statement statement = null;

        try {
            connection =
DriverManager.getConnection("jdbc:mysql://localhost:3306/mydb", "root",
"password");
            connection.setAutoCommit(false);
            statement = connection.createStatement();

            statement.addBatch("INSERT INTO users (username, age) VALUES
('alice', 25)");
            statement.addBatch("INSERT INTO users (username, age) VALUES
('bob', 28)");

            int[] result = statement.executeBatch();
            connection.commit();
            System.out.println(result.length + " rows inserted.");
        } catch (SQLException e) {
            e.printStackTrace();
        } finally {
            try {
                if (statement != null) statement.close();
                if (connection != null) connection.close();
            } catch (SQLException e) {
                e.printStackTrace();
            }
        }
    }
}
```

Output:

```
2 rows inserted.
```

Puzzle 71: ResultSet Iteration

Problem: Demonstrate iteration through a `ResultSet`.

```java
import java.sql.*;

public class ResultSetIterationExample {
    public static void main(String[] args) {
        Connection connection = null;
        Statement statement = null;

        try {
            connection =
DriverManager.getConnection("jdbc:mysql://localhost:3306/mydb", "root",
"password");
            statement = connection.createStatement();
            ResultSet resultSet = statement.executeQuery("SELECT * FROM
users");

            while (resultSet.next()) {
                System.out.println("ID: " + resultSet.getInt("id") + ",
Username: " + resultSet.getString("username"));
            }
        } catch (SQLException e) {
            e.printStackTrace();
        } finally {
            try {
                if (statement != null) statement.close();
                if (connection != null) connection.close();
            } catch (SQLException e) {
                e.printStackTrace();
            }
        }
    }
}
```

Output:

```
ID: 1, Username: john_doe
ID: 2, Username: alice
```

Puzzle 72: Transaction Handling

Problem: Demonstrate transaction handling with JDBC.

```java
import java.sql.*;

public class TransactionExample {
    public static void main(String[] args) {
        Connection connection = null;
        Statement statement = null;
```

```java
        try {
            connection =
DriverManager.getConnection("jdbc:mysql://localhost:3306/mydb", "root",
"password");
            connection.setAutoCommit(false);
            statement = connection.createStatement();

            statement.executeUpdate("UPDATE users SET age = 30 WHERE id =
1");
            // Simulate an error
            int result = 1 / 0; // ArithmeticException
            statement.executeUpdate("UPDATE users SET age = 35 WHERE id =
2");

            connection.commit();
            System.out.println("Transaction committed.");
        } catch (Exception e) {
            try {
                connection.rollback();
                System.out.println("Transaction rolled back.");
            } catch (SQLException ex) {
                ex.printStackTrace();
            }
        } finally {
            try {
                if (statement != null) statement.close();
                if (connection != null) connection.close();
            } catch (SQLException e) {
                e.printStackTrace();
            }
        }
    }
}
```

Output:

Puzzle 73: CallableStatement

Problem: Demonstrate the use of `CallableStatement` for calling stored procedures in JDBC.

```java
import java.sql.*;

public class CallableStatementExample {
    public static void main(String[] args) {
        Connection connection = null;
        CallableStatement callableStatement = null;

        try {
            connection =
DriverManager.getConnection("jdbc:mysql://localhost:3306/mydb", "root",
"password");
            String sql = "{CALL getUserById(?)}";
```

```
            callableStatement = connection.prepareCall(sql);
            callableStatement.setInt(1, 1);

            ResultSet resultSet = callableStatement.executeQuery();
            while (resultSet.next()) {
                System.out.println("ID: " + resultSet.getInt("id") + ",
Username: " + resultSet.getString("username"));
            }
        } catch (SQLException e) {
            e.printStackTrace();
        } finally {
            try {
                if (callableStatement != null) callableStatement.close();
                if (connection != null) connection.close();
            } catch (SQLException e) {
                e.printStackTrace();
            }
        }
    }
}
```

Output:

```
ID: 1, Username: john_doe
```

Puzzle 74: Handling NULL Values in ResultSet

Problem: Demonstrate how to handle NULL values in a `ResultSet`.

```
import java.sql.*;

public class NullValueHandlingExample {
    public static void main(String[] args) {
        Connection connection = null;
        Statement statement = null;

        try {
            connection =
DriverManager.getConnection("jdbc:mysql://localhost:3306/mydb", "root",
"password");
            statement = connection.createStatement();
            ResultSet resultSet = statement.executeQuery("SELECT * FROM
users");

            while (resultSet.next()) {
                String username = resultSet.getString("username");
                if (resultSet.wasNull()) {
                    System.out.println("Username is NULL.");
                } else {
                    System.out.println("Username: " + username);
                }
            }
        } catch (SQLException e) {
```

```
            e.printStackTrace();
        } finally {
            try {
                if (statement != null) statement.close();
                if (connection != null) connection.close();
            } catch (SQLException e) {
                e.printStackTrace();
            }
        }
    }
}
```

Output:

```
Username: john_doe
Username is NULL.
```

Puzzle 75: Auto-Commit Mode

Problem: Demonstrate the effect of auto-commit mode in JDBC.

```
import java.sql.*;

public class AutoCommitExample {
    public static void main(String[] args) {
        Connection connection = null;
        Statement statement = null;

        try {
            connection =
DriverManager.getConnection("jdbc:mysql://localhost:3306/mydb", "root",
"password");
            connection.setAutoCommit(true);
            statement = connection.createStatement();
            statement.executeUpdate("UPDATE users SET age = 30 WHERE id =
1");

            System.out.println("Auto-commit is enabled. Changes are
automatically committed.");
        } catch (SQLException e) {
            e.printStackTrace();
        } finally {
            try {
                if (statement != null) statement.close();
                if (connection != null) connection.close();
            } catch (SQLException e) {
                e.printStackTrace();
            }
        }    }}
```

Output:

```
Auto-commit is enabled. Changes are automatically committed.
```

Puzzle 76: Handling SQLException

Problem: Demonstrate handling `SQLException` with a custom error message.

```java
import java.sql.*;

public class SQLExceptionHandlingExample {
    public static void main(String[] args) {
        Connection connection = null;

        try {
            connection =
DriverManager.getConnection("jdbc:mysql://localhost:3306/nonexistentdb",
"root", "password");
        } catch (SQLException e) {
            System.out.println("Error: " + e.getMessage());
        } finally {
            try {
                if (connection != null) connection.close();
            } catch (SQLException e) {
                e.printStackTrace();
            }
        }
    }
}
```

Output:

```
Error: Communications link failure
```

Puzzle 77: JSP Page Lifecycle

Problem: Demonstrate the lifecycle methods of a JSP page.

```jsp
<%@ page language="java" contentType="text/html; charset=ISO-8859-1"%>
<%@ page import="java.util.Date" %>
<html>
<head>
    <title>JSP Lifecycle</title>
</head>
<body>
    <h2>JSP Lifecycle Methods</h2>
    <p>Current Date and Time: <%= new Date() %></p>
</body>
</html>
```

Solution: This JSP page demonstrates the use of the page's lifecycle method, where the new Date() object is created when the page is requested, and the page is reloaded on each request, showing the current date and time.

Puzzle 78: JSP Directives

Problem: Use a directive in a JSP to specify the content type of the response.

```
<%@ page contentType="text/html; charset=UTF-8" %>
<html>
<head>
    <title>JSP Content Type</title>
</head>
<body>
    <h2>Content Type Demonstration</h2>
    <p>This page is served with content type UTF-8 encoding.</p>
</body>
</html>
```

Solution: The directive `<%@ page contentType="text/html; charset=UTF-8" %>` sets the content type for the response to `UTF-8`, which ensures proper encoding of characters.

Puzzle 79: JSP Implicit Objects

Problem: Demonstrate the use of implicit objects like `request` and `response` in JSP.

```
<%@ page import="java.util.*" %>
<html>
<head>
    <title>JSP Implicit Objects</title>
</head>
<body>
    <h2>JSP Implicit Objects Example</h2>
    <%
        String userName = request.getParameter("name");
        out.println("Hello, " + userName);
    %>
    <form action="" method="GET">
        Name: <input type="text" name="name">
        <input type="submit" value="Submit">
    </form>
</body>
</html>
```

Solution: The `request` implicit object is used to fetch the value of a query parameter (`name`), and the `out` implicit object is used to send a response to the browser.

Puzzle 80: JSP Expression Language (EL)

Problem: Demonstrate the use of JSP Expression Language (EL) to print variables.

```
<%@ page language="java" contentType="text/html; charset=ISO-8859-1" %>
<html>
<head>
    <title>JSP EL Example</title>
</head>
<body>
    <h2>JSP Expression Language</h2>
    <p>Hello, ${param.name}!</p>
</body>
</html>
```

Solution: In this JSP, EL is used to access request parameters directly by the `${param.name}` syntax, making the code more readable and reducing scriptlets.

Puzzle 81: JSP Error Handling

Problem: Demonstrate error handling in JSP using the `errorPage` directive.

```
<%@ page errorPage="errorPage.jsp" %>
<html>
<head>
    <title>Error Handling in JSP</title>
</head>
<body>
    <h2>JSP Error Handling</h2>
    <%
        int result = 10 / 0; // This will throw an ArithmeticException
    %>
</body>
</html>
```

Solution: The `errorPage` directive points to `errorPage.jsp` when an error occurs. Any exception thrown in the JSP will be forwarded to this page.

Puzzle 82: JSP Forwarding

Problem: Demonstrate forwarding from one JSP page to another.

```
<%@ page language="java" contentType="text/html; charset=ISO-8859-1" %>
<%@ page import="java.io.*" %>
<%
    RequestDispatcher dispatcher =
request.getRequestDispatcher("anotherPage.jsp");
```

```
        dispatcher.forward(request, response);
%>
```

Solution: This example demonstrates how to forward a request from one JSP page to another using the `RequestDispatcher.forward()` method.

Puzzle 83: JSP Include Directive

Problem: Demonstrate the use of the `include` directive in JSP.

```
<%@ include file="header.jsp" %>
<html>
<head>
    <title>JSP Include Directive</title>
</head>
<body>
    <h2>Using Include Directive in JSP</h2>
    <p>This content includes the header.jsp page.</p>
</body>
</html>
```

Solution: The `include` directive is used to include the content of the `header.jsp` file into the current JSP page during translation.

Puzzle 84: JSP Custom Tags

Problem: Demonstrate the use of a simple custom tag in JSP.

```
<%@ taglib uri="http://java.sun.com/jsp/jstl/core" prefix="c" %>
<html>
<head>
    <title>Custom Tag Example</title>
</head>
<body>
    <h2>Using JSTL Tags</h2>
    <c:out value="${param.name}" />
</body>
</html>
```

Solution: This JSP uses JSTL's `<c:out>` tag to print the value of a request parameter named `name`, avoiding scriptlets and improving readability.

Puzzle 85: JSP Cookie Handling

Problem: Demonstrate reading and setting cookies in a JSP page.

```jsp
Copy code
<%@ page import="javax.servlet.http.*" %>
<%
    // Setting a cookie
    Cookie userCookie = new Cookie("username", "JohnDoe");
    response.addCookie(userCookie);

    // Reading cookies
    Cookie[] cookies = request.getCookies();
    if (cookies != null) {
        for (Cookie cookie : cookies) {
            if ("username".equals(cookie.getName())) {
                out.println("Hello, " + cookie.getValue());
            }
        }
    }
%>
```

Solution: This JSP page sets a cookie for `username` and retrieves it from the request to display a personalized greeting.

Puzzle 86: Servlet Initialization

Problem: Demonstrate how to initialize a servlet using the `init()` method.

```java
import javax.servlet.*;
import java.io.*;

public class InitServlet extends GenericServlet {
    public void init() {
        System.out.println("Servlet initialized");
    }

    public void service(ServletRequest req, ServletResponse res) throws
ServletException, IOException {
        PrintWriter out = res.getWriter();
        out.println("Hello from Servlet!");
    }
}
```

Solution: The `init()` method is called when the servlet is first loaded into memory, allowing for initialization tasks.

Puzzle 87: Servlet Config

Problem: Use `ServletConfig` to pass initialization parameters to the servlet.

```
import javax.servlet.*;
import java.io.*;

public class ConfigServlet extends GenericServlet {
    public void service(ServletRequest req, ServletResponse res) throws
ServletException, IOException {
        ServletConfig config = getServletConfig();
        String username = config.getInitParameter("username");
        PrintWriter out = res.getWriter();
        out.println("Username from init parameter: " + username);
    }
}
```

Solution: `ServletConfig` is used to retrieve initialization parameters specified in the `web.xml` file.

Puzzle 88: Servlet Context

Problem: Demonstrate the use of `ServletContext` to share data between servlets.

```
import javax.servlet.*;
import java.io.*;

public class ContextServlet extends GenericServlet {
    public void service(ServletRequest req, ServletResponse res) throws
ServletException, IOException {
        ServletContext context = getServletContext();
        context.setAttribute("appName", "MyApp");

        PrintWriter out = res.getWriter();
        out.println("Application name: " + context.getAttribute("appName"));
    }
}
```

Solution: `ServletContext` allows servlets to share attributes across the application.

Puzzle 89: Servlet Mapping

Problem: Demonstrate how to map a servlet to a URL pattern using `web.xml`.

```
<web-app>
    <servlet>
        <servlet-name>MyServlet</servlet-name>
```

```
        <servlet-class>MyServlet</servlet-class>
    </servlet>
    <servlet-mapping>
        <servlet-name>MyServlet</servlet-name>
        <url-pattern>/myservlet</url-pattern>
    </servlet-mapping>
</web-app>
```

Solution: This `web.xml` configuration maps the `MyServlet` to the `/myservlet` URL pattern.

Puzzle 90: Servlet Request Parameters

Problem: Demonstrate how to retrieve query parameters from a servlet.

```
import javax.servlet.*;
import java.io.*;

public class RequestParamServlet extends GenericServlet {
    public void service(ServletRequest req, ServletResponse res) throws
ServletException, IOException {
        String name = req.getParameter("name");
        PrintWriter out = res.getWriter();
        out.println("Hello, " + name);
    }}
```

Solution: The `getParameter()` method is used to retrieve query parameters passed in the request URL.

Puzzle 91: Servlet Response Types

Problem: Set the content type of the response in a servlet.

```
import javax.servlet.*;
import java.io.*;

public class ContentTypeServlet extends GenericServlet {
    public void service(ServletRequest req, ServletResponse res) throws
ServletException, IOException {
        res.setContentType("text/html");

        PrintWriter out = res.getWriter();
        out.println("<html><body><h2>Hello from
Servlet!</h2></body></html>");
    }}
```

Solution: The `setContentType()` method specifies the type of response (e.g., `text/html`).

Puzzle 92: Servlet Handling POST Request

Problem: Handle POST requests in a servlet.

```
import javax.servlet.*;
import javax.servlet.http.*;
import java.io.*;

public class PostServlet extends HttpServlet {
    protected void doPost(HttpServletRequest req, HttpServletResponse res)
throws ServletException, IOException {
        String username = req.getParameter("username");
        PrintWriter out = res.getWriter();
        out.println("Hello, " + username);
    }
}
```

Solution: The `doPost()` method is overridden to handle POST requests. The form parameter is retrieved using `getParameter()`.

Puzzle 93: Servlet Handling GET Request

Problem: Handle GET requests in a servlet.

```
import javax.servlet.*;
import javax.servlet.http.*;
import java.io.*;

public class GetServlet extends HttpServlet {
    protected void doGet(HttpServletRequest req, HttpServletResponse res)
throws ServletException, IOException {
        String message = "This is a GET request";
        PrintWriter out = res.getWriter();
        out.println(message);
    }
}
```

Solution: The `doGet()` method is overridden to handle GET requests. The response is printed using a `PrintWriter`.

Puzzle 94: Servlet Session Management

Problem: Create a servlet that manages session attributes.

```
import javax.servlet.*;
import javax.servlet.http.*;
import java.io.*;
```

```
public class SessionServlet extends HttpServlet {
    protected void doGet(HttpServletRequest req, HttpServletResponse res)
throws ServletException, IOException {
        HttpSession session = req.getSession();
        session.setAttribute("user", "JohnDoe");

        PrintWriter out = res.getWriter();
        out.println("User session attribute set: " +
session.getAttribute("user"));
    }
}
```

Solution: This servlet creates a session and stores a user attribute. The session is retrieved using getSession() and the attribute is set with setAttribute().

Puzzle 95: Servlet Redirection

Problem: Demonstrate how to redirect a request to another URL using sendRedirect().

```
import javax.servlet.*;
import javax.servlet.http.*;
import java.io.*;

public class RedirectServlet extends HttpServlet {
    protected void doGet(HttpServletRequest req, HttpServletResponse res)
throws ServletException, IOException {
        res.sendRedirect("https://www.example.com");
    }
}
```

Solution: The sendRedirect() method is used to redirect the response to another URL.

Puzzle 96: Simple TCP Server and Client Communication

Problem: Write a simple TCP server and client program where the client sends a message to the server, and the server responds with a confirmation message. **Server Code:**

```
import java.io.*;
import java.net.*;

public class SimpleServer {
    public static void main(String[] args) throws IOException {
        ServerSocket serverSocket = new ServerSocket(1234);
        System.out.println("Server started... waiting for connections...");
        Socket clientSocket = serverSocket.accept();
        PrintWriter out = new PrintWriter(clientSocket.getOutputStream(),
true);
        BufferedReader in = new BufferedReader(new
InputStreamReader(clientSocket.getInputStream()));
```

```
            String message = in.readLine();
            System.out.println("Client says: " + message);
            out.println("Message received: " + message);

            clientSocket.close();
            serverSocket.close();
        }
    }
}
```

Client Code:

```
import java.io.*;
import java.net.*;

public class SimpleClient {
    public static void main(String[] args) throws IOException {
        Socket socket = new Socket("localhost", 1234);
        PrintWriter out = new PrintWriter(socket.getOutputStream(), true);
        BufferedReader in = new BufferedReader(new
InputStreamReader(socket.getInputStream()));

        out.println("Hello Server!");
        System.out.println("Server says: " + in.readLine());

        socket.close();
    }
}
```

Solution: The client sends a message to the server, and the server responds with a confirmation message.

Puzzle 97: Multithreaded Server

Problem: Create a multithreaded server that handles multiple clients. **Server Code:**

```
import java.io.*;
import java.net.*;

public class MultiThreadedServer {
    public static void main(String[] args) throws IOException {
        ServerSocket serverSocket = new ServerSocket(1234);
        System.out.println("Server started... waiting for connections...");

        while (true) {
            Socket clientSocket = serverSocket.accept();
            new ClientHandler(clientSocket).start();
        }
    }
}

class ClientHandler extends Thread {
```

```
        private Socket clientSocket;

        public ClientHandler(Socket socket) {
            this.clientSocket = socket;
        }

        public void run() {
            try {
                PrintWriter out = new PrintWriter(clientSocket.getOutputStream(),
true);
                BufferedReader in = new BufferedReader(new
InputStreamReader(clientSocket.getInputStream()));

                String message = in.readLine();
                out.println("Server received: " + message);

                clientSocket.close();
            } catch (IOException e) {
                e.printStackTrace();
            }
        }
    }
}
```

Solution: This multithreaded server can handle multiple client connections by creating a new thread for each client.

Puzzle 98: Echo Server

Problem: Create a simple echo server where the client sends a message, and the server responds by echoing the same message. **Server Code:**

```
import java.io.*;
import java.net.*;

public class EchoServer {
    public static void main(String[] args) throws IOException {
        ServerSocket serverSocket = new ServerSocket(1234);
        System.out.println("Echo Server started... waiting for
connections...");

        Socket clientSocket = serverSocket.accept();
        BufferedReader in = new BufferedReader(new
InputStreamReader(clientSocket.getInputStream()));
        PrintWriter out = new PrintWriter(clientSocket.getOutputStream(),
true);

        String message;
```

```
        while ((message = in.readLine()) != null) {
            out.println("Echo: " + message);
        }

        clientSocket.close();
        serverSocket.close();
    }
}
```

Client Code:

```
import java.io.*;
import java.net.*;

public class EchoClient {
    public static void main(String[] args) throws IOException {
        Socket socket = new Socket("localhost", 1234);
        BufferedReader in = new BufferedReader(new
InputStreamReader(socket.getInputStream()));
        PrintWriter out = new PrintWriter(socket.getOutputStream(), true);

        out.println("Hello, Server!");
        System.out.println("Server: " + in.readLine());

        socket.close();
    }
}
```

Solution: The server echoes back any message it receives from the client.

Puzzle 99: UDP Communication

Problem: Create a simple UDP server and client that exchange messages. **Server Code:**

```
import java.net.*;

public class UDPServer {
    public static void main(String[] args) throws Exception {
        DatagramSocket socket = new DatagramSocket(1234);
        byte[] receiveData = new byte[1024];

        while (true) {
            DatagramPacket receivePacket = new DatagramPacket(receiveData,
receiveData.length);
            socket.receive(receivePacket);
            String message = new String(receivePacket.getData(), 0,
receivePacket.getLength());
            System.out.println("Received from client: " + message);

            InetAddress clientAddress = receivePacket.getAddress();
            int clientPort = receivePacket.getPort();
            String response = "Message received";
```

```
              DatagramPacket sendPacket = new
DatagramPacket(response.getBytes(), response.length(), clientAddress,
clientPort);
              socket.send(sendPacket);
          }
      }
}
```

Client Code:

```
import java.net.*;

public class UDPClient {
    public static void main(String[] args) throws Exception {
        DatagramSocket socket = new DatagramSocket();
        String message = "Hello, UDP Server!";
        DatagramPacket sendPacket = new DatagramPacket(message.getBytes(),
message.length(), InetAddress.getByName("localhost"), 1234);
        socket.send(sendPacket);

        byte[] receiveData = new byte[1024];
        DatagramPacket receivePacket = new DatagramPacket(receiveData,
receiveData.length);
        socket.receive(receivePacket);
        System.out.println("Server: " + new String(receivePacket.getData(),
0, receivePacket.getLength()));

        socket.close();
    }
}
```

Solution: This example demonstrates basic communication using UDP, where the server receives a message and sends a response.

Puzzle 100: File Transfer via Socket

Problem: Transfer a file from client to server using TCP sockets. **Server Code:**

```
import java.io.*;
import java.net.*;

public class FileTransferServer {
    public static void main(String[] args) throws IOException {
        ServerSocket serverSocket = new ServerSocket(1234);
        Socket clientSocket = serverSocket.accept();
        InputStream inputStream = clientSocket.getInputStream();
        FileOutputStream fileOutputStream = new
FileOutputStream("received_file.txt");

        byte[] buffer = new byte[1024];
        int bytesRead;
        while ((bytesRead = inputStream.read(buffer)) != -1) {
```

```
            fileOutputStream.write(buffer, 0, bytesRead);
        }

        fileOutputStream.close();
        inputStream.close();
        clientSocket.close();
        serverSocket.close();
    }
}
```

Client Code:

```java
import java.io.*;
import java.net.*;

public class FileTransferClient {
    public static void main(String[] args) throws IOException {
        Socket socket = new Socket("localhost", 1234);
        FileInputStream fileInputStream = new
FileInputStream("send_file.txt");
        OutputStream outputStream = socket.getOutputStream();

        byte[] buffer = new byte[1024];
        int bytesRead;
        while ((bytesRead = fileInputStream.read(buffer)) != -1) {
            outputStream.write(buffer, 0, bytesRead);
        }

        fileInputStream.close();
        outputStream.close();
        socket.close();      }}
```

Solution: The client sends a file to the server using TCP sockets, and the server saves the received data to a file.

Interview Insight:

1. **Question:** What is the difference between ArrayList and LinkedList in Java? **Answer:** ArrayList provides fast random access, but slow insertions and deletions, while LinkedList provides fast insertions and deletions but slower access time due to its node-based structure.
2. **Question:** What is the use of the final keyword in Java? **Answer:** The final keyword can be used to define constants, prevent method overriding, and prevent inheritance of classes.
3. **Question:** What is the difference between == and equals() in Java? **Answer:** == checks for reference equality (if both references point to the same object), while equals() checks for value equality (if the objects are logically equivalent).
4. **Question:** What is the purpose of hashCode() method in Java? **Answer:** The hashCode() method is used to provide a unique identifier for objects, which is important in hash-based collections like HashMap and HashSet.

5. **Question:** What are the differences between synchronized and volatile in Java? **Answer:** synchronized ensures thread safety by allowing only one thread to access a block of code at a time, while volatile ensures that changes to a variable are visible to all threads immediately.

6. **Question:** What is the use of transient keyword in Java? **Answer:** The transient keyword is used to indicate that a field should not be serialized when the object is serialized.

7. **Question:** What is the difference between String, StringBuilder, and StringBuffer? **Answer:** String is immutable, StringBuilder is mutable and not thread-safe, and StringBuffer is mutable and thread-safe.

8. **Question:** What is an exception in Java, and how is it handled? **Answer:** An exception is an event that disrupts the normal flow of execution. It is handled using try, catch, and finally blocks.

9. **Question:** What is the difference between checked and unchecked exceptions in Java? **Answer:** Checked exceptions are exceptions that must be explicitly handled or declared, while unchecked exceptions (runtime exceptions) are not mandatory to handle.

10. **Question:** What is the difference between ArrayList and Vector in Java? **Answer:** ArrayList is not synchronized and has better performance, while Vector is synchronized and may have performance overhead in multi-threaded environments.

11. **Question:** What is the super keyword in Java? **Answer:** The super keyword refers to the superclass of the current object and is used to access superclass methods and constructors.

12. **Question:** What is the this keyword in Java? **Answer:** The this keyword refers to the current object and is used to distinguish instance variables from local variables with the same name.

13. **Question:** What are the differences between String and StringBuilder? **Answer:** String is immutable, meaning its value cannot be changed once created, while StringBuilder is mutable, allowing modifications without creating new objects.

14. **Question:** What is method overloading in Java? **Answer:** Method overloading is defining multiple methods with the same name but different parameters (either in number, type, or both) in a class.

15. **Question:** What is method overriding in Java? **Answer:** Method overriding is defining a method in the subclass that has the same signature as a method in the superclass, providing specific behavior for the subclass.

16. **Question:** What is the difference between final, finally, and finalize in Java? **Answer:** final is used for constants, methods, and classes; finally is used to define a block of code that will always execute after a try block; finalize is a method used to clean up resources before an object is garbage collected.

17. **Question:** What is the difference between throw and throws in Java? **Answer:** throw is used to explicitly throw an exception in a method, while throws is used to declare that a method may throw certain exceptions.

18. **Question:** What is the purpose of the default keyword in interfaces? **Answer:** The default keyword allows a method to have a default implementation in an interface, introduced in Java 8.

19. **Question:** What is a constructor in Java? **Answer:** A constructor is a special method used to initialize objects. It has the same name as the class and is called when an object is created.

20. **Question:** What is the difference between Runnable and Thread in Java? **Answer:** Runnable is an interface that defines a run() method, while Thread is a class that represents a thread of execution. A Runnable can be passed to a Thread object to create a thread.

21. **Question:** What is the difference between int and Integer in Java? **Answer:** int is a primitive data type, while Integer is a wrapper class that encapsulates an int value and provides additional methods.

22. **Question:** What is a static variable in Java? **Answer:** A static variable is a variable that belongs to the class rather than any instance of the class, meaning it is shared among all objects of the class.

23. **Question:** What is the difference between ArrayList and LinkedList in terms of performance? **Answer:** ArrayList is faster for random access operations, while LinkedList is more efficient for insertions and deletions.

24. **Question:** What is the Iterator interface in Java? **Answer:** The Iterator interface provides methods to iterate over a collection, including hasNext(), next(), and remove().

25. **Question:** What are functional interfaces in Java? **Answer:** A functional interface is an interface with just one abstract method, used primarily for lambda expressions.

26. **Question:** What is the purpose of clone() method in Java? **Answer:** The clone() method is used to create a copy of an object, usually a shallow copy unless overridden in the class.

27. **Question:** What is a package in Java? **Answer:** A package is a namespace that groups related classes and interfaces, providing access control and namespace management.

28. **Question:** What is the difference between Comparable and Comparator in Java? **Answer:** Comparable defines a natural ordering for objects, whereas Comparator defines an external comparison strategy.

29. **Question:** What is the difference between ArrayList and LinkedList in terms of memory usage? **Answer:** ArrayList uses a contiguous block of memory, while LinkedList uses additional memory for each node to store references to the previous and next nodes.

30. **Question:** What are the different types of inner classes in Java? **Answer:** Java supports four types of inner classes: regular inner class, static nested class, local inner class, and anonymous class.

31. **Question:** What is the StringBuilder class used for? **Answer:** StringBuilder is used to create mutable strings, which can be modified without creating new objects, improving performance in string manipulations.

32. **Question:** What is the Serializable interface in Java? **Answer:** The Serializable interface is used to mark a class whose objects can be serialized, allowing them to be converted into a byte stream for storage or transmission.

33. **Question:** What is a synchronized block in Java? **Answer:** A synchronized block is used to ensure that only one thread can access a block of code at a time, ensuring thread safety.

34. **Question:** What is the difference between StringBuilder and StringBuffer? **Answer:** Both are used to create mutable strings, but StringBuilder is not synchronized, while StringBuffer is synchronized for thread safety.

35. **Question:** What is the use of instanceof operator in Java? **Answer:** The instanceof operator checks if an object is an instance of a particular class or implements a particular interface.

36. **Question:** What is a default method in Java interfaces? **Answer:** A default method in an interface provides a default implementation that can be overridden by implementing classes.

37. **Question:** What is the purpose of super() constructor in Java? **Answer:** The super() constructor is used to call the constructor of the superclass from the subclass.

38. **Question:** What are the main differences between Set and List in Java? **Answer:** Set does not allow duplicate elements and does not guarantee order, while List allows duplicates and maintains the order of insertion.

39. **Question:** What is a Map in Java? **Answer:** A Map is a collection of key-value pairs, where each key is unique and maps to a specific value.

40. **Question:** What is the difference between HashMap and TreeMap in Java? **Answer:** HashMap is unordered and allows null keys, while TreeMap is ordered according to the natural ordering of keys or by a comparator.

41. **Question:** What is the purpose of finally block in Java? **Answer:** The finally block is used to execute code that must run regardless of whether an exception is thrown or not, often used for cleanup tasks.

42. **Question:** What is the difference between StringBuffer and StringBuilder? **Answer:** StringBuffer is synchronized and thread-safe, while StringBuilder is not synchronized and is faster in single-threaded environments.

43. **Question:** What is the difference between public, protected, and private access modifiers in Java? **Answer:** public allows access from any class, protected allows access within the same package or subclasses, and private restricts access to the current class only.

44. **Question:** What is the purpose of the volatile keyword in Java? **Answer:** The volatile keyword ensures that changes to a variable are immediately visible to all threads, preventing issues with caching.

45. **Question:** What is a singleton class in Java? **Answer:** A singleton class ensures that only one instance of the class exists throughout the application.

46. **Question:** What is the difference between == and equals() when comparing objects in Java? **Answer:** == compares memory references (if both refer to the same object), while equals() compares the actual content of objects for equality.

47. **Question:** What is a try-with-resources statement in Java? **Answer:** A try-with-resources statement automatically closes resources like files or database connections after the try block is executed.

48. **Question:** What is the difference between public static void main(String[] args) and public static void main(String... args)? **Answer:** Both methods are equivalent, but String... args allows passing a variable number of arguments, while String[] args is a fixed array of strings.

49. **Question:** What is an abstract class in Java? **Answer:** An abstract class is a class that cannot be instantiated and may contain abstract methods that must be implemented by subclasses.

50. **Question:** What is the Thread.sleep() method in Java? **Answer:** The Thread.sleep() method pauses the execution of the current thread for a specified amount of time.

51. **Question:** What is the difference between final, finally, and finalize in Java? **Answer:** final is used to define constants, prevent method overriding, and prevent inheritance of classes; finally is used to define a block of code that will always execute after a try block; finalize is used to define cleanup operations before an object is garbage collected.

52. **Question:** What is the purpose of the assert keyword in Java? **Answer:** The assert keyword is used to test assumptions in code during development, helping to detect logical errors. Assertions are typically disabled at runtime.

53. **Question:** What is the difference between == and equals() for comparing strings in Java? **Answer:** == compares the memory references of two strings, whereas equals() compares the actual content of the strings.

54. **Question:** What are lambda expressions in Java? **Answer:** Lambda expressions are a feature introduced in Java 8 that allow you to pass behavior (a function or block of code) as a parameter to methods, making code more concise and readable.

55. **Question:** What is a NullPointerException in Java, and how can you avoid it? **Answer:** A NullPointerException occurs when trying to access or modify an object that is null. It can be avoided by checking for null values before using objects.

56. **Question:** What is the purpose of the super() constructor call in Java? **Answer:** super() is used to call the constructor of the superclass from a subclass, ensuring proper initialization of the inherited fields.

57. **Question:** What is the difference between synchronized methods and synchronized blocks in Java? **Answer:** Synchronized methods lock the entire method, while synchronized blocks allow finer control, locking only the specific code block rather than the entire method.

58. **Question:** What is a deadlock in Java? **Answer:** A deadlock occurs when two or more threads are blocked forever, waiting for each other to release resources. It can be avoided by ensuring proper locking order.

59. **Question:** What is the String.intern() method in Java? **Answer:** The intern() method is used to add a string to the string pool. If the string already exists in the pool, it returns the reference to the pooled instance; otherwise, it adds the string to the pool.

60. **Question:** What is the difference between notify() and notifyAll() in Java? **Answer:** notify() wakes up one thread that is waiting on the object's monitor, while notifyAll() wakes up all threads waiting on the object's monitor.

61. **Question:** What is the role of wait() in Java synchronization? **Answer:** The wait() method is used by a thread to release the lock and enter the waiting state until notified by another thread via notify() or notifyAll().

62. **Question:** What is a try-catch block in Java? **Answer:** A try-catch block is used for exception handling. The code that may throw an exception is placed in the try block, and the exception is handled in the catch block.

63. **Question:** What are the differences between List and Set interfaces in Java? **Answer:** List allows duplicate elements and maintains order, while Set does not allow duplicates and does not guarantee order.

64. **Question:** What is a checked exception in Java? **Answer:** A checked exception is a type of exception that must either be caught or declared in the method signature using throws.

65. **Question:** What is a unchecked exception in Java? **Answer:** An unchecked exception is a type of exception that does not need to be explicitly caught or declared, and typically extends RuntimeException.

66. **Question:** What is an anonymous class in Java? **Answer:** An anonymous class is a class without a name, defined at the point of instantiation, typically used to implement interfaces or extend classes.

67. **Question:** What is a constructor in Java? **Answer:** A constructor is a special method used to initialize objects. It has the same name as the class and is called automatically when an object is created.

68. **Question:** What is a static method in Java? **Answer:** A static method is a method that belongs to the class rather than an instance of the class, and it can be called without creating an object of the class.

69. **Question:** What is the purpose of this() in Java constructors? **Answer:** this() is used to call another constructor in the same class, enabling constructor chaining.

70. **Question:** What is the Default method in Java interfaces? **Answer:** A default method in an interface provides a default implementation, allowing interfaces to evolve without breaking existing implementations.

71. **Question:** What is the difference between StringBuilder and StringBuffer? **Answer:** Both are used for mutable strings, but StringBuilder is not thread-safe, while StringBuffer is synchronized and thread-safe.

72. **Question:** What is a package in Java? **Answer:** A package is a namespace used to organize related classes and interfaces, helping in code maintenance and avoiding name conflicts.

73. **Question:** What is the instanceof operator in Java? **Answer:** The instanceof operator checks whether an object is an instance of a specified class or interface.

74. **Question:** What are the access modifiers in Java? **Answer:** Java provides four access modifiers: public, protected, private, and default (no modifier), which control the visibility of classes, methods, and fields.

75. **Question:** What is a constructor overloading in Java? **Answer:** Constructor overloading is a concept where a class has multiple constructors with different parameter lists to initialize objects in various ways.

76. **Question:** What is Garbage Collection in Java? **Answer:** Garbage collection is the process by which Java automatically clears memory by reclaiming unused objects, thus preventing memory leaks.

77. **Question:** What is the purpose of the main() method in Java? **Answer:** The main() method is the entry point of a Java program. It is where the execution begins, and it must be declared as public static void main(String[] args).

78. **Question:** What is a hashCode() function in Java? **Answer:** The hashCode() function returns a unique integer identifier for an object, used by hash-based collections like HashMap and HashSet for efficient lookups.

79. **Question:** What is a Map in Java? **Answer:** A Map is a collection that stores key-value pairs, where each key is unique and maps to a value.

80. **Question:** What is a TreeMap in Java? **Answer:** A TreeMap is a Map implementation that stores key-value pairs in sorted order based on the natural ordering of keys or a custom comparator.

81. **Question:** What is a ThreadPoolExecutor in Java? **Answer:** ThreadPoolExecutor is a class that provides a flexible mechanism for managing a pool of worker threads for executing tasks concurrently.

82. **Question:** What is the final keyword used for in Java? **Answer:** The final keyword is used to declare constants, prevent method overriding, and prevent inheritance of a class.

83. **Question:** What is a volatile variable in Java? **Answer:** A volatile variable ensures that changes to a variable are immediately visible to all threads, preventing thread-local caching of its value.

84. **Question:** What is the Thread.join() method in Java? **Answer:** The join() method allows one thread to wait for the completion of another thread before continuing its execution.

85. **Question:** What is the difference between ArrayList and LinkedList in Java? **Answer:** ArrayList provides faster random access and is more efficient for search operations, while LinkedList is more efficient for insertions and deletions.

86. **Question:** What is synchronized keyword in Java? **Answer:** The synchronized keyword ensures that only one thread can access a method or block of code at a time, providing thread safety.

87. **Question:** What is an Enum in Java? **Answer:** An Enum is a special type that defines a set of constants, typically representing a fixed set of related values.

88. **Question:** What is a singleton pattern in Java? **Answer:** A singleton pattern ensures that only one instance of a class exists in the application and provides a global point of access to it.

89. **Question:** What is the purpose of the super keyword in Java? **Answer:** The super keyword is used to refer to the superclass of the current object, allowing access to superclass methods, constructors, and fields.

90. **Question:** What is the Iterable interface in Java? **Answer:** The Iterable interface represents a collection of objects that can be iterated using an iterator. It defines a single method iterator().

91. **Question:** What is an interface in Java? **Answer:** An interface is a contract that defines a set of abstract methods which must be implemented by any class that chooses to implement the interface.

92. **Question:** What is the default method in an interface in Java? **Answer:** A default method in an interface provides a default implementation, allowing new methods to be added to interfaces without breaking existing implementations.

93. **Question:** What is throws in Java? **Answer:** The throws keyword is used in method declarations to specify that a method can throw exceptions, making the caller aware of the potential exceptions.

94. **Question:** What is a break statement in Java? **Answer:** The break statement is used to exit a loop or a switch statement prematurely.

95. **Question:** What is a continue statement in Java? **Answer:** The continue statement is used to skip the current iteration of a loop and move to the next iteration.

96. **Question:** What is the difference between String and StringBuilder in terms of performance? **Answer:** String is immutable, so concatenating strings creates new objects each time, leading to performance overhead, while StringBuilder is mutable and provides better performance for string manipulation.

97. **Question:** What is a reentrant lock in Java? **Answer:** A reentrant lock allows the thread that holds the lock to re-acquire it without getting blocked, useful for preventing deadlocks.

98. **Question:** What is the purpose of the finalize() method in Java? **Answer:** The finalize() method is called before an object is garbage collected, providing a chance to clean up resources or perform any final tasks.

99. **Question:** What is Collection in Java? **Answer:** Collection is a root interface in the Java Collections Framework, representing a group of objects, with sub-interfaces like Set, List, and Queue.

100. **Question:** What is the Iterator pattern in Java? **Answer:** The Iterator pattern provides a way to access elements of a collection sequentially without exposing the underlying structure of the collection. It is implemented via the Iterator interface in Java.

101. **Question:** What is the difference between ArrayList and Vector in Java? **Answer:** ArrayList is not synchronized and generally provides better performance in single-threaded environments, while Vector is synchronized and is thread-safe, but its performance is slower compared to ArrayList.

102. **Question:** What are Map.Entry and how is it used in Java? **Answer:** Map.Entry is a nested interface in the Map interface representing a key-value pair. It is used in iterating over the elements of a Map.

103. **Question:** What is a WeakReference in Java? **Answer:** A WeakReference allows the referenced object to be garbage collected when it is no longer in use, unlike strong references which prevent garbage collection.

104. **Question:** What are Set and SortedSet in Java? **Answer:** Set is an interface that does not allow duplicate elements, while SortedSet is a subinterface of Set that maintains elements in a sorted order.

105. **Question:** What is the difference between Iterator and ListIterator in Java? **Answer:** Iterator is used for traversing a Collection in one direction (forward), while ListIterator extends Iterator and allows bidirectional traversal of a List.

106. **Question:** What is a ThreadLocal variable in Java? **Answer:** ThreadLocal is a class that provides thread-local variables, which means each thread accessing them has its own independent copy of the variable.

107. **Question:** What is the significance of the transient keyword in Java? **Answer:** The transient keyword is used to mark a variable as not to be serialized when the object is written to a stream.

108. **Question:** What is the difference between sleep() and wait() in Java? **Answer:** sleep() pauses the current thread for a specified time without releasing any locks, while wait() causes the current thread to release the lock and enter the waiting state until notified.

109. **Question:** What is the difference between StringBuilder and StringBuffer in Java? **Answer:** StringBuilder is not synchronized and is faster for single-threaded environments, while StringBuffer is synchronized and is thread-safe, making it slower compared to StringBuilder.

110. **Question:** What is the use of the super keyword in Java? **Answer:** The super keyword refers to the immediate superclass of the current object and is used to access superclass methods, constructors, and fields.

111. **Question:** What is a final class in Java? **Answer:** A final class is a class that cannot be subclassed. This is useful to prevent inheritance and ensure that the class remains unchanged.

112. **Question:** What is the difference between HashMap and TreeMap in Java? **Answer:** HashMap stores key-value pairs in an unordered fashion, while TreeMap stores key-value pairs in a sorted order based on the keys.

113. **Question:** What is the use of the default method in Java interfaces? **Answer:** The default method provides a default implementation in an interface, which can be overridden by implementing classes if needed.

114. **Question:** What is a Cloneable interface in Java? **Answer:** The Cloneable interface is used to indicate that a class supports cloning, allowing objects to be copied using the clone() method.

115. **Question:** What is the finalize() method in Java? **Answer:** The finalize() method is called by the garbage collector before an object is destroyed, allowing it to perform cleanup operations.

116. **Question:** What is the difference between Object and Class in Java? **Answer:** Object is the root class for all classes in Java, while Class is a representation of a class type itself, allowing you to get metadata about the class.

117. **Question:** What is the use of Thread.sleep() in Java? **Answer:** Thread.sleep() pauses the execution of the current thread for a specified amount of time, allowing other threads to execute.

118. **Question:** What is the difference between ArrayList and LinkedList in Java? **Answer:** ArrayList uses a dynamic array for storing elements, providing faster random access but slower insertions, while LinkedList uses a doubly linked list, providing faster insertions and deletions but slower access.

119. **Question:** What is the volatile keyword in Java? **Answer:** The volatile keyword ensures that changes to a variable are immediately visible to all threads, preventing thread-local caching.

120. **Question:** What is the purpose of the System.currentTimeMillis() method in Java? **Answer:** The System.currentTimeMillis() method returns the current time in milliseconds from the epoch (January 1, 1970), commonly used for measuring elapsed time.

121. **Question:** What is an Interface in Java? **Answer:** An interface defines a contract that classes can implement. It specifies methods without providing implementation, allowing different classes to provide their own versions of those methods.

122. **Question:** What is the Runtime class in Java? **Answer:** The Runtime class allows access to the Java runtime environment, providing methods to interact with the system, like memory management and executing system commands.

123. **Question:** What is the assert statement in Java? **Answer:** The assert statement is used to test assumptions during runtime and helps identify errors. It is disabled by default and can be enabled through the JVM.

124. **Question:** What is the purpose of instanceof in Java? **Answer:** The instanceof operator checks whether an object is an instance of a specified class or subclass.

125. **Question:** What are the Map methods in Java? **Answer:** Common methods in the Map interface include put(), get(), remove(), containsKey(), and containsValue(), among others, for manipulating key-value pairs.

126. **Question:** What is the Observer design pattern in Java? **Answer:** The Observer design pattern defines a one-to-many dependency between objects, where one object (the subject) notifies others (observers) of any state changes.

127. **Question:** What is the use of the break statement in Java? **Answer:** The break statement is used to exit from a loop or switch statement prematurely.

128. **Question:** What is the continue statement in Java? **Answer:** The continue statement skips the current iteration of a loop and proceeds to the next iteration.

129. **Question:** What is the difference between Runnable and Thread in Java? **Answer:** Runnable is a functional interface that represents a task that can be executed by a thread, while Thread is a class that represents an actual thread of execution. A thread can execute a Runnable task.

130. **Question:** What is the Comparator interface in Java? **Answer:** The Comparator interface is used to define a custom order for objects of a class, providing a method compare() to compare two objects.

131. **Question:** What is the difference between ArrayList and HashSet in Java? **Answer:** ArrayList allows duplicates and maintains insertion order, while HashSet does not allow duplicates and does not guarantee any specific order.

132. **Question:** What is the purpose of the super() constructor call in Java? **Answer:** The super() constructor call is used to invoke the constructor of the parent class to initialize inherited properties.

133. **Question:** What is the Callable interface in Java? **Answer:** The Callable interface represents a task that can be executed asynchronously, similar to Runnable, but it can return a result or throw an exception.

134. **Question:** What is the difference between throw and throws in Java? **Answer:** throw is used to throw an exception explicitly from within a method, while throws is used in a method declaration to indicate that a method might throw an exception.

135. **Question:** What is the EnumSet in Java? **Answer:** EnumSet is a specialized Set implementation for use with Enum types. It is more efficient than a regular HashSet when working with enums.

136. **Question:** What is the purpose of Objects.equals() in Java? **Answer:** The Objects.equals() method provides a null-safe way to check if two objects are equal, preventing NullPointerException when either object is null.

137. **Question:** What is the difference between notify() and notifyAll() in Java? **Answer:** notify() wakes up a single thread waiting on the object's monitor, while notifyAll() wakes up all threads waiting on the object's monitor.

138. **Question:** What is java.util.Optional in Java? **Answer:** Optional is a container object which may or may not contain a value. It is used to prevent NullPointerException by explicitly handling null values.

139. **Question:** What is a synchronized block in Java? **Answer:** A synchronized block is used to restrict access to a specific block of code, ensuring that only one thread can execute it at a time.

140. **Question:** What is HashMap in Java? **Answer:** HashMap is a class that implements the Map interface, storing key-value pairs in a hash table. It allows fast lookup and retrieval of elements based on the key.

141. **Question:** What is the difference between final and const in Java? **Answer:** final is a keyword that defines constants or prevents method overriding and class inheritance, while const is not used in Java.

142. **Question:** What is the Java Memory Model (JMM)? **Answer:** The Java Memory Model (JMM) defines how threads interact with memory and how variables are read and written in a multithreaded environment to ensure consistency and visibility.

143. **Question:** What is the difference between == and .equals() for object comparison in Java? **Answer:** == compares memory references, while .equals() compares the actual contents or state of objects.

144. **Question:** What is the difference between Serializable and Externalizable interfaces in Java? **Answer:** Serializable is a marker interface used for object serialization, while Externalizable allows full control over the serialization process by defining the writeExternal() and readExternal() methods.

145. **Question:** What is the default keyword in Java interfaces? **Answer:** The default keyword allows methods in interfaces to have default implementations, enabling backward compatibility while adding new methods.

146. **Question:** What is java.nio package in Java? **Answer:** The java.nio package provides classes for non-blocking input/output operations, including buffers, channels, and selectors for more efficient file and network I/O.

147. **Question:** What is the difference between String and StringBuffer in Java? **Answer:** String is immutable, meaning its value cannot be changed after it is created, while StringBuffer is mutable and allows modification of the string content.

148. **Question:** What is the role of the equals() method in Java?

Answer: The equals() method is used to compare the contents of two objects for equality. By default, it compares memory addresses, but it can be overridden for logical comparisons.

149. **Question:** What is the purpose of the hashCode() method in Java?

Answer: The hashCode() method provides a hash code for an object, used by hashing-based collections like HashMap and HashSet to store and retrieve objects efficiently.

150. **Question:** What is the difference between LinkedList and ArrayList in Java?

Answer: ArrayList uses a dynamic array to store elements, providing faster access but slower insertions. LinkedList uses a doubly linked list, providing faster insertions but slower access.

151. **Question:** What are synchronized methods in Java?

Answer: Synchronized methods are used to control access to a block of code by multiple threads, ensuring that only one thread can execute the method at a time.

152. **Question:** What is the final keyword used for in Java?

Answer: The final keyword is used to declare constants, prevent method overriding, and prevent inheritance of a class.

153. **Question:** What is a deadlock in Java?

Answer: A deadlock is a situation in which two or more threads are blocked forever because they are waiting for each other to release resources.

154. **Question:** What is the try-catch block in Java?

Answer: The try-catch block is used to handle exceptions in Java. Code that might throw an exception is placed inside the try block, and the catch block handles the exception.

155. **Question:** What is the use of the super() constructor in Java?

Answer: super() is used to invoke the constructor of the superclass, allowing the initialization of inherited properties.

156. **Question:** What is the difference between ArrayList and LinkedList in terms of performance?

Answer: ArrayList provides faster access and search performance (O(1)) but slower insertions and deletions (O(n)), while LinkedList provides faster insertions and deletions (O(1)) but slower access and search performance (O(n)).

157. **Question:** What is a Map in Java?

Answer: A Map is a collection that stores key-value pairs. It does not allow duplicate keys and provides fast lookups based on the key.

158. **Question:** What is the Thread class in Java?

Answer: The Thread class represents a thread of execution in Java. It provides methods to start, pause, and stop a thread.

159. **Question:** What are the advantages of using Vector in Java?

Answer: Vector is a thread-safe collection, and it can dynamically resize as elements are added. However, it is generally slower than ArrayList due to synchronization overhead.

160. **Question:** What is a Lambda expression in Java?

Answer: A Lambda expression is a concise way to represent an anonymous function (or method) that can be passed as an argument to a method or assigned to a variable.

161. **Question:** What is a Stream in Java?

Answer: A Stream is a sequence of elements supporting sequential and parallel aggregate operations, introduced in Java 8, that allows functional-style operations on collections.

162. **Question:** What is a MethodReference in Java?

Answer: A MethodReference is a shorthand notation for calling a method using a lambda expression. It refers directly to a method without invoking it.

163. **Question:** What is the Runnable interface in Java?

Answer: The Runnable interface represents a task that can be executed by a thread. It contains a single run() method, which defines the task to be performed.

164. **Question:** What is the purpose of System.exit() in Java?

Answer: System.exit() is used to terminate the Java Virtual Machine (JVM) and the program with a specific exit status code.

165. **Question:** What is the difference between ArrayList and HashSet in Java?

Answer: ArrayList maintains insertion order and allows duplicates, whereas HashSet does not maintain order and does not allow duplicates.

166. **Question:** What is synchronization in Java?

Answer: Synchronization in Java is used to prevent multiple threads from accessing the same resource concurrently, ensuring thread safety.

167. **Question:** What is the equals() and hashCode() contract in Java?

Answer: The equals() and hashCode() methods should be consistent. If two objects are equal according to equals(), they must have the same hash code.

168. **Question:** What is java.util.Date in Java?

Answer: java.util.Date represents a specific instant in time, with millisecond precision. It is often used to handle date and time information.

169. **Question:** What are the types of exceptions in Java?

Answer: Exceptions in Java are divided into two categories: checked exceptions (which must be handled) and unchecked exceptions (which do not need to be explicitly handled).

170. **Question:** What is the use of the throw keyword in Java?

Answer: The throw keyword is used to explicitly throw an exception from a method or block of code.

171. **Question:** What is the NullPointerException in Java?

Answer: NullPointerException occurs when an application attempts to use an object reference that has not been initialized (null).

172. **Question:** What is the difference between == and .equals() for comparing objects in Java?

Answer: == compares references or memory addresses of objects, while .equals() compares the content or state of the objects.

173. **Question:** What is the Comparator interface in Java?

Answer: The Comparator interface is used to define custom ordering for objects, providing a method compare() to compare two objects.

174. **Question:** What is the Enum in Java?

Answer: Enum is a special class in Java that represents a group of constants (unchangeable variables), providing type safety and a more readable way to handle fixed sets of values.

175. **Question:** What is a final method in Java?

Answer: A final method in Java cannot be overridden by subclasses, ensuring that the method's implementation remains unchanged.

176. **Question:** What is the ThreadPoolExecutor class in Java?

Answer: ThreadPoolExecutor is a class in the java.util.concurrent package that manages a pool of worker threads to execute tasks concurrently.

177. **Question:** What is the use of volatile keyword in Java?

Answer: The volatile keyword ensures that a variable's value is always read from and written to the main memory, providing visibility across threads.

178. **Question:** What is the Callable interface in Java?

Answer: Callable is a functional interface similar to Runnable, but it can return a result or throw an exception, and it is used with ExecutorService.

179. **Question:** What is the difference between wait() and sleep() in Java?

Answer: wait() releases the lock on the object and puts the thread in a waiting state until notified, while sleep() pauses the thread for a specific time without releasing any locks.

180. **Question:** What is the ExecutorService in Java?

Answer: ExecutorService is an interface for managing and controlling thread execution in concurrent Java applications, providing methods like submit() and shutdown().

181. **Question:** What is the ForkJoinPool in Java?

Answer: ForkJoinPool is a specialized implementation of ExecutorService designed for parallel programming, where tasks can be recursively split into smaller tasks for parallel execution.

182. **Question:** What is java.nio in Java?

Answer: java.nio is a package that provides non-blocking I/O operations using buffers, channels, and selectors, which help in efficient file and network I/O.

183. **Question:** What is the LinkedHashMap in Java?

Answer: LinkedHashMap is a Map implementation that maintains the order of insertion of key-value pairs. It combines the functionality of HashMap and a linked list.

184. **Question:** What is the Stream API in Java 8?

Answer: The Stream API is used for processing sequences of elements in a functional style, supporting operations like filter, map, and reduce, which can be applied to collections.

185. **Question:** What is the Optional class in Java?

Answer: The Optional class is used to represent a value that may or may not be present, helping to avoid NullPointerException by explicitly handling absence of values.

186. **Question:** What is a synchronized block in Java?

Answer: A synchronized block is used to restrict access to a block of code, ensuring that only one thread can execute it at a time, typically used to control concurrent access to a shared resource.

187. **Question:** What is the Reflection API in Java?

Answer: The Reflection API allows inspecting and manipulating classes, methods, and fields at runtime, enabling dynamic behavior in Java programs.

188. **Question:** What is the @Override annotation in Java?

Answer: The @Override annotation indicates that a method is overriding a method from its superclass, helping the compiler to check for errors and improve code readability.

189. **Question:** What is the volatile keyword in Java?

Answer: The volatile keyword is used to indicate that a variable's value can be changed by multiple threads. It ensures that the latest value of the variable is always visible to all threads.

190. **Question:** Explain synchronized keyword in Java.

Answer: The synchronized keyword is used to control access to a block of code or method to ensure that only one thread can execute it at a time, preventing race conditions.

191. **Question:** What are the different types of class loaders in Java?

Answer: The three types of class loaders in Java are:

Bootstrap ClassLoader – Loads core Java classes.

Extension ClassLoader – Loads classes from the JRE's lib/ext directory.

System ClassLoader – Loads classes from the classpath.

192. **Question:** What is the difference between notify() and notifyAll() in Java?

Answer: notify() wakes up one thread that is waiting on the object's monitor, while notifyAll() wakes up all the threads that are waiting.

193. **Question:** What are Callable and Runnable interfaces?

Answer: Runnable is used to represent a task that can be executed by a thread but doesn't return any result. Callable is similar to Runnable but returns a result and can throw exceptions.

194. **Question:** What is the ForkJoinPool in Java?

Answer: ForkJoinPool is a specialized implementation of ExecutorService designed to work with parallel tasks that can be recursively broken into smaller subtasks, useful for divide-and-conquer algorithms.

195. **Question:** What is the difference between StringBuilder and StringBuffer?

Answer: Both StringBuilder and StringBuffer are used to create mutable strings. The difference is that StringBuffer is synchronized and thread-safe, while StringBuilder is not, making it faster in single-threaded scenarios.

196. **Question:** What is the transient keyword used for in Java?

Answer: The transient keyword is used to indicate that a field should not be serialized. When an object is serialized, any field marked as transient is excluded from the serialization process.

197. **Question:** What is the use of the instanceof keyword in Java?

Answer: The instanceof keyword is used to test whether an object is an instance of a particular class or interface.

198. **Question:** What are default methods in interfaces?

Answer: Introduced in Java 8, default methods allow interfaces to have concrete methods with a default implementation. This helps in extending interfaces without breaking existing implementations.

199. **Question:** What is the purpose of the static keyword in Java?

Answer: The static keyword is used to define class-level variables and methods that can be accessed without creating an instance of the class.

200. **Question:** What is the difference between final, finally, and finalize in Java?

Answer:

- final is used to define constants, prevent method overriding, and prevent inheritance.
- finally is used to define a block of code that will always execute after a try block.
- finalize() is a method in Object class that is invoked before an object is garbage collected.

CHAPTER-2

Mock Interview Problems with Solutions

Mock interview problems help candidates simulate real interview scenarios. They typically consist of various problem categories that assess the candidate's proficiency in core programming concepts, debugging skills, system design knowledge, and algorithmic thinking. Here's a detailed explanation of three common types of mock interview problems:

End-to-End Problems from Coding Rounds

End-to-end problems in coding rounds are comprehensive challenges designed to test a candidate's ability to apply a wide range of concepts from data structures, algorithms, software design, and coding practices to solve real-world problems. These problems often require candidates to:

1. **Understand the Problem Domain:** This involves thoroughly reading and interpreting the problem statement, understanding the requirements, constraints, and expected behavior of the system.
2. **Design the Algorithm:** Based on the understanding of the problem, the candidate must design an efficient algorithm. This step may involve deciding the approach, selecting appropriate data structures, and thinking about time and space complexities.
3. **Write Efficient Code:** Writing code that implements the algorithm in a clean, efficient manner is the next step. This includes making sure the code is modular, follows coding best practices, and solves the problem correctly.
4. **Testing Edge Cases:** It is essential to test the solution with various edge cases, such as empty inputs, very large inputs, or corner cases that may expose weaknesses in the algorithm or implementation.
5. **Optimize for Time and Space Complexity:** After writing the solution, it is important to consider its time and space complexity. Optimizing the algorithm for better performance, especially with respect to large input sizes, is a key step in coding rounds.

Example Problem: Design a URL Shortener

Problem Statement:
You are tasked with designing a URL shortener service (like bit.ly). The system should allow a user to shorten a given URL and retrieve the original URL from the shortened version.

Requirements:

1. When given a URL, return a shortened URL.
2. When given a shortened URL, retrieve the original URL.

Design Approach

1. **Generate a Unique ID for Each URL:**
   - The core of the URL shortening service is to convert a long URL into a short one. The shortest form of a URL typically involves generating a unique identifier for the original URL.
   - One way to do this is by using a **hash function** to map the original URL to a unique identifier.
   - A simple approach is to use the hash code of the URL (though this can lead to collisions).
   - Alternatively, more advanced approaches involve **base62 encoding**, which encodes numbers into a set of alphanumeric characters (a-z, A-Z, 0-9). This gives a wider range of unique identifiers.

2. **Store the Mapping:**
   - We will need a **database or a data structure** (like a `HashMap`) to store the mapping between the shortened URL (unique ID) and the original URL.
   - This mapping allows us to efficiently retrieve the original URL when a shortened URL is provided.

3. **Retrieve the Original URL:**
   - When a user provides a shortened URL, we can extract the unique identifier from the URL and query the mapping to retrieve the original URL.

Solution:

Here's how we can implement the solution in Java:

```java
import java.util.HashMap;

public class URLShortener {
    private HashMap<String, String> urlMap; // Map to store the shortened URL
and the original URL
    private String baseURL; // Base URL for shortening

    // Constructor initializes the URL map and base URL
    public URLShortener() {
        urlMap = new HashMap<>();
        baseURL = "http://short.ly/"; // The base URL used for shortening
    }

    // Method to generate a short URL from the original URL
    public String shortenURL(String originalURL) {
        // Generate a unique hash for the original URL (use hashCode and
convert to hex string)
        String shortURL = Integer.toHexString(originalURL.hashCode());

        // Store the mapping of shortened URL to the original URL
        urlMap.put(shortURL, originalURL);

        // Return the full shortened URL
        return baseURL + shortURL;
```

```java
}

    // Method to retrieve the original URL from the shortened URL
    public String getOriginalURL(String shortURL) {
        // Extract the key (the unique hash) from the shortened URL
        String key = shortURL.replace(baseURL, "");

        // Retrieve and return the original URL from the map
        return urlMap.get(key);
    }

    public static void main(String[] args) {
        URLShortener shortener = new URLShortener();

        // Original URL
        String originalURL = "https://www.example.com";

        // Shorten the URL
        String shortURL = shortener.shortenURL(originalURL);
        System.out.println("Shortened URL: " + shortURL);

        // Retrieve the original URL using the shortened URL
        String retrievedURL = shortener.getOriginalURL(shortURL);
        System.out.println("Original URL: " + retrievedURL);
    }
}
```

Explanation of Code:

- **Class Variables:**
    - urlMap: A HashMap that stores the mapping of shortened URLs to original URLs.
    - baseURL: The base URL that is used to prepend the shortened hash string, forming the complete shortened URL.
- **Methods:**
    - shortenURL(String originalURL): This method accepts an original URL, generates a unique shortened URL by converting the hash code of the original URL into a hexadecimal string, stores the mapping in the urlMap, and returns the complete shortened URL.
    - getOriginalURL(String shortURL): This method accepts a shortened URL, extracts the unique identifier (hash), and retrieves the original URL from the urlMap.
- **Main Method:**
    - It demonstrates how to shorten a URL and retrieve the original URL using the implemented methods.

Edge Cases and Considerations:

1. **Collision Handling:**
   - Hash collisions can occur when two different URLs produce the same hash code. In such cases, two different URLs will be mapped to the same shortened URL. This could be problematic. One way to mitigate this issue is by using a more sophisticated hash function or using base62 encoding for uniqueness.
   - Another solution could be to check if the hash already exists in the map, and if so, regenerate the hash or use a counter (a unique ID generator).
2. **Invalid Shortened URL Input:**
   - We assume that the shortened URL provided by the user is always valid. In real-world systems, we must add validation to ensure that the shortened URL is correctly formatted, and its mapping exists in the database. This can be done by checking if the hash exists in the `urlMap`.
3. **URL Length Limitations:**
   - Depending on the system, there might be restrictions on the length of the URL. For instance, the URL might need to fit within a certain length for it to be considered valid.
4. **Security Considerations:**
   - In a real-world application, URL shorteners may expose some form of security risk. For example, malicious actors might shorten URLs to redirect users to harmful sites. Security checks should be implemented to verify the integrity of the destination URL before shortening it.

Optimization:

1. **Time Complexity:**
   - **Shortening URL:** The `shortenURL()` method performs a `hashCode()` operation and stores the mapping in a `HashMap`. Both operations take constant time, i.e., **O(1)**.
   - **Retrieving URL:** The `getOriginalURL()` method retrieves the original URL from the `HashMap`, which is also an **O(1)** operation.
2. **Space Complexity:**
   - The space complexity is **O(n)**, where n is the number of unique URLs stored. This is because each URL is stored in the `urlMap`.

By considering the design, approach, and edge cases, this end-to-end problem tests a candidate's understanding of algorithms, data structures, and their ability to write efficient, scalable code.

---

2. Debugging Challenges

Debugging challenges are designed to evaluate a candidate's ability to identify and fix bugs in a given piece of code. These problems test the candidate's knowledge of common programming issues, their debugging skills, and their ability to reason through the code's behavior while keeping the intended functionality intact. The key skills required for debugging challenges include:

1. **Identifying Bugs**: Spotting errors in logic, incorrect assumptions, improper usage of data structures, and mistakes in syntax or variable handling.
2. **Fixing Bugs**: Applying appropriate fixes while ensuring the code remains functional and efficient. This often involves understanding how the program should behave, finding the root cause of the issue, and making necessary changes.
3. **Understanding Code Flow**: Analyzing the control flow and state of the program at different points to understand why it isn't working as expected.
4. **Testing and Verifying**: Ensuring that the bug fix does not introduce new errors and the solution works under various input conditions.

Example Problem: Fix the Bug in Sorting Algorithm

Problem Statement:

You are given a sorting algorithm that does not return the correct sorted list. Your task is to identify the bug and fix it.

Here's the **buggy code**:

```java
import java.util.List;

public class BuggySort {
    public static void buggySort(List<Integer> nums) {
        for (int i = 0; i < nums.size(); i++) {
            for (int j = i + 1; j < nums.size(); j++) {
                if (nums.get(i) > nums.get(j)) {
                    int temp = nums.get(i);
                    nums.set(i, nums.get(j));
                    nums.set(j, temp);
                }
            }
        }
    }

    public static void main(String[] args) {
        List<Integer> nums = List.of(5, 2, 9, 1, 5, 6);
        buggySort(nums);
        System.out.println("Sorted List: " + nums);
    }
}
```

Bug Explanation:

- **The Issue**: The code tries to sort a list of integers using a bubble sort algorithm. However, it fails because the list is immutable. In Java, the method `List.of()` creates an immutable list, meaning that the list cannot be modified (e.g., using `nums.set(i, value)`).

- When the code attempts to modify the list using `nums.set(i, ...)`, it throws an `UnsupportedOperationException` because the list returned by `List.of()` does not support modification.

Solution:

To fix this, we need to use a **mutable list**. A simple solution is to replace the immutable list with a mutable list (e.g., `ArrayList`). This will allow us to modify the list using methods like `set()`.

Here's the **fixed code**:

```java
import java.util.ArrayList;
import java.util.List;

public class BuggySort {
    public static void buggySort(List<Integer> nums) {
        for (int i = 0; i < nums.size(); i++) {
            for (int j = i + 1; j < nums.size(); j++) {
                if (nums.get(i) > nums.get(j)) {
                    int temp = nums.get(i);
                    nums.set(i, nums.get(j));
                    nums.set(j, temp);
                }
            }
        }
    }

    public static void main(String[] args) {
        // Use a mutable ArrayList instead of the immutable List created by
List.of()
        List<Integer> nums = new ArrayList<>(List.of(5, 2, 9, 1, 5, 6));

        // Call the buggySort method to sort the list
        buggySort(nums);

        // Print the sorted list
        System.out.println("Sorted List: " + nums);
    }
}
```

Explanation of Fix:

- The key change here is that we replaced `List.of()` with `new ArrayList<>(List.of(...))`. This converts the immutable list created by `List.of()` into a mutable `ArrayList`, which can be modified using `set()` to swap elements during sorting.
- Once the list is mutable, the sorting algorithm can successfully modify the list, and the sorting works as intended.

Edge Cases Considered:

1. **Empty List**: If the input list is empty, the algorithm will not perform any swaps, and the list remains empty.

2. **Single Element**: If the input list contains only one element, the algorithm will not make any swaps, and the list remains unchanged.
3. **Duplicate Elements**: The algorithm will work with duplicate elements as well, ensuring that the list is sorted correctly, including handling duplicates in their correct positions.

Time Complexity:

- The time complexity of the sorting algorithm is **O(n²)** due to the two nested loops (a classic characteristic of bubble sort).

Space Complexity:

- The space complexity is **O(1)**, as the sorting is done in place without any additional data structures.

Key Takeaways for Debugging Challenges:

1. **Understand the Code Context:**
   - Always begin by understanding the intended functionality of the code. In this case, the goal was to sort a list of integers. Knowing what the code is trying to accomplish helps you identify why it fails.
2. **Check for Common Bugs:**
   - Common issues in debugging challenges include problems with **mutable vs immutable data structures, incorrect algorithm implementation, off-by-one errors**, and **incorrect edge case handling**. Identifying these issues quickly can help fix the problem faster.
3. **Use Test Cases:**
   - It's always important to test the code with a variety of inputs, including edge cases, to ensure that the solution works for all scenarios. Here, testing with empty lists, single-element lists, and lists with duplicates would be essential.
4. **Efficient Debugging:**
   - Break down the code logically and analyze its flow. When debugging, think about the variables, their values, and how they change throughout the execution. In this case, recognizing that the list is immutable and cannot be modified was the key insight.

By practicing debugging challenges, candidates can improve their problem-solving and coding skills, especially when faced with unexpected bugs in the code.

---

3. System Design Problems for Java Developers

System design problems are crucial for testing a candidate's ability to design large-scale, scalable, and efficient systems. These problems often require candidates to consider various aspects such as performance, scalability, availability, fault tolerance, maintainability, and consistency. Unlike coding challenges that focus on specific algorithms or data structures, system design problems assess the candidate's ability to handle real-world problems involving multiple components, services, and interactions.

Key Aspects of System Design:

1. **Scalability**: The system should be able to handle increasing amounts of load (e.g., more requests, larger datasets) without significant performance degradation.
2. **Performance**: Systems need to respond quickly, even under high load. This often requires techniques such as caching, load balancing, and distributed systems.
3. **Availability**: The system should remain operational even in the face of partial failures. This requires redundancy, replication, and fault tolerance.
4. **Maintainability**: The system should be easy to monitor, troubleshoot, and scale over time.
5. **Fault Tolerance**: The system should continue to function even if parts of it fail, using techniques like redundancy, retries, and graceful degradation.

Example Problem: Design a Distributed Caching System

A distributed caching system improves the performance of an application by reducing database load. It stores frequently accessed data in a fast-access memory (cache). In this problem, we are tasked with designing such a system with the following requirements:

Problem Requirements:

1. **Cache with multiple nodes**: The system must handle multiple cache nodes distributed across servers.
2. **Cache misses**: If the data is not in the cache (a "cache miss"), it should be fetched from the main database.
3. **LRU (Least Recently Used) eviction policy**: When the cache reaches its maximum capacity, the least recently accessed data should be evicted.

Design Components:

1. **Cache Nodes**:
   o Multiple servers holding the cached data in memory.
   o Each cache node is responsible for a portion of the data (sharding).
2. **Database**:
   o A persistent storage layer (e.g., relational database or NoSQL database) to store the main data.
3. **Cache Manager**:
   o A layer that manages caching logic: handling cache misses, distributing data, and evicting data from the cache.
   o This layer can also implement sharding (dividing the cache into segments) to distribute data across multiple cache nodes.
4. **Sharding**:
   o The cache is split into smaller segments and distributed across multiple cache nodes. This ensures that no single node becomes overwhelmed.

5. **LRU Eviction**:
   o Each cache node will implement the **LRU eviction policy**. If the cache exceeds its capacity, the least recently used item is removed.
6. **Data Synchronization**:
   o If a cache node lacks a certain piece of data, it can fetch the data from the database and store it in the local cache for future use.

Solution Implementation in Java:

In Java, a simple approach to implementing the LRU eviction policy can be achieved using `LinkedHashMap`. This data structure maintains the order of insertion and allows for easy eviction based on the least recently accessed entry.

Code Example:
```java
import java.util.LinkedHashMap;
import java.util.Map;

public class DistributedCache {
    private final int capacity;
    private final Map<String, String> cache;

    public DistributedCache(int capacity) {
        this.capacity = capacity;
        // LinkedHashMap maintains insertion order, and with 'true' as the
3rd argument, it keeps access order.
        this.cache = new LinkedHashMap<>(capacity, 0.75f, true);
    }

    // Retrieve value from cache or fetch from the database if not found
    public String get(String key) {
        if (cache.containsKey(key)) {
            return cache.get(key);  // Return cached value
        }
        return fetchFromDatabase(key);  // Fetch from database on cache miss
    }

    // Insert value into cache and evict if necessary
    public void put(String key, String value) {
        if (cache.size() >= capacity) {
            evict();  // Evict least recently used item if cache is full
        }
        cache.put(key, value);  // Insert new value into cache
    }

    // Simulate fetching data from the database
    private String fetchFromDatabase(String key) {
        // In a real-world scenario, replace this with actual database
queries
        return "Database Value for " + key;
    }

    // Evicts the least recently used (LRU) entry
    private void evict() {
```

```
        // LinkedHashMap maintains insertion order, and the first entry is
the least recently accessed
        String firstKey = cache.keySet().iterator().next();
        cache.remove(firstKey);   // Evict the first (least recently accessed)
entry
    }

    public static void main(String[] args) {
        DistributedCache cache = new DistributedCache(3);   // Cache capacity
is 3
        cache.put("A", "1");
        cache.put("B", "2");
        cache.put("C", "3");

        System.out.println(cache.get("A"));   // Should print "1"
        cache.put("D", "4");
        System.out.println(cache.get("B"));   // Should print "Database Value
for B" as B was evicted
    }
}
```

Explanation of the Code:

1. **LinkedHashMap for LRU Policy**:
   o The LinkedHashMap is used with the third argument set to true to maintain access order. This allows us to easily evict the least recently accessed entry by simply removing the first entry.
2. **Cache Operations**:
   o **get(String key)**: Checks if the key is present in the cache. If present, returns the cached value. If not, it simulates a database fetch.
   o **put(String key, String value)**: Inserts data into the cache. If the cache exceeds its capacity, it calls the evict() method to remove the least recently used item.
   o **evict()**: Evicts the least recently used item by removing the first entry in the LinkedHashMap.
3. **Database Simulation**:
   o The fetchFromDatabase method simulates retrieving data from a persistent database (in practice, this could be a network call to a database system).
4. **Testing**:
   o After inserting items "A", "B", and "C" into the cache, we retrieve "A", then insert "D", which causes "B" to be evicted because it was the least recently used.

Challenges in Distributed Caching Systems:

1. Cache Synchronization

Cache synchronization refers to ensuring that the data stored in multiple cache nodes is consistent and up-to-date. When a system consists of several distributed cache nodes, each node may have a part of the data, and changes in one node need to be reflected in others to maintain consistency.

Challenges of Cache Synchronization:

- **Cache Misses and Eviction**: When a cache node evicts an item, it may be removed from memory, but another node or the database might still contain the data. If a request for the evicted item is made, it must be fetched from the other cache node or the database, which can introduce delays.
- **Consistency**: In a distributed cache, different nodes may have different versions of the data due to updates, evictions, or network latency. Ensuring that all cache nodes reflect the same data at any given time becomes a challenge, particularly in high-traffic systems.

Strategies to Address Cache Synchronization:

- **Cache Invalidation**: A method where all cache nodes are notified to invalidate their local copy of the data when it is updated in one of the nodes. This way, when a node requests the data, it is forced to fetch it from the primary source (database or other nodes).
- **Write-through and Write-behind Caching**: In a write-through cache, every write operation is immediately reflected in the main database and all cache nodes. In write-behind, the cache update happens asynchronously, and synchronization is handled periodically.
- **Consistent Hashing**: This technique helps in distributing data uniformly across cache nodes and ensures that when nodes are added or removed, the cache synchronization is less disruptive.

Example: If a key-value pair ("user1", "data1") is evicted from one cache node, but another node or the database has the same data, a cache miss will trigger a fetch from either the other node or the database. Ensuring that all nodes have a consistent version of the data during such operations is key to maintaining system reliability.

---

2. Scaling

As the system grows and more data is stored, scaling the cache system to handle larger amounts of data while maintaining high performance becomes increasingly complex. This challenge typically involves:

- **Horizontal Scaling**: Adding more cache nodes to handle increased load. This requires distributing data across multiple nodes (sharding) and ensuring that the data is efficiently distributed and accessed.
- **Vertical Scaling**: Adding more resources (CPU, RAM) to existing cache nodes to increase their capacity. However, vertical scaling has physical limits, and it doesn't solve issues like load balancing and fault tolerance.

Challenges of Scaling:

- **Data Distribution**: As the cache size increases, data distribution becomes more complex. Simple sharding strategies may not be sufficient. Techniques like consistent hashing or partitioning ensure that data is distributed evenly across multiple cache nodes, and when a node fails or is added, minimal data is disrupted.
- **Load Balancing**: As the number of nodes increases, the load on each cache node must be balanced effectively. If one node is handling more requests than others, it may lead to latency and poor system performance. Proper load balancing strategies are necessary.
- **Latency**: With more nodes, data may need to travel across the network, which can introduce latency. Optimizing network calls and reducing the round-trip time for cache lookups are crucial.

Solution for Scaling:

- **Sharding**: Split the cache into smaller, manageable chunks (shards) and distribute them across nodes. Each shard can store a specific range of data, and each node will be responsible for a subset of the total data.
- **Consistent Hashing**: This technique helps minimize disruption when scaling out or in. Consistent hashing ensures that only a few data points are relocated when a node is added or removed, reducing the need to reshard all the data.

3. Replication

Replication in a cache system involves creating copies of data across multiple nodes to ensure availability and fault tolerance. When one node fails, another node with a replica of the data can continue to serve the requests.

Challenges of Replication:

- **Consistency**: In replicated cache systems, the data across the replicated nodes may become inconsistent due to network partitions or delays in updating replicas. When one node updates its data, it must ensure that all other replicas are updated promptly, which can lead to performance overhead.
- **Write Propagation**: When data is updated in one replica, it needs to be propagated to all other replicas to maintain consistency. This process needs to be efficient, and the system must decide whether updates should be synchronous (all replicas must update before acknowledging) or asynchronous (replicas can update independently).
- **Latency**: Replication can increase latency because requests may need to go through multiple copies of data to ensure the latest version is available. If the system is configured to use strong consistency, it may need to wait for all replicas to update before returning a response.

CHAPTER-3

Java Coding Test Preparation

Preparing for Java coding tests, particularly for interviews or competitive programming, involves focused practice on problem-solving, algorithmic thinking, and mastering the Java programming language. Below are detailed strategies for each of the key aspects of Java coding test preparation.

1. Timed Practice Questions

Timed practice is a critical component of coding test preparation, as it mirrors the real-world constraints of competitive programming and coding interviews. The key goal is to improve your speed and accuracy while maintaining a methodical approach to solving problems.

Purpose of Timed Practice

Timed practice simulates the actual conditions you'll face during coding tests or competitive programming events, where you are expected to solve problems within a limited time frame. Here's a deeper dive into its importance:

Why Timed Practice Is Important

1. **Time Management**:
   - **Critical for Coding Tests**: In coding tests, whether in an interview or a competitive environment, you typically face a limited amount of time to solve each problem. This makes time management essential to ensuring that you can solve problems efficiently and within the given time constraints.
   - **Developing Efficiency**: Through timed practice, you'll learn how to divide your available time wisely between reading the problem, designing an algorithm, writing code, and debugging. Over time, you'll develop the ability to prioritize tasks effectively and allocate time appropriately to each phase of problem-solving.
2. **Stress Handling**:
   - **Real-World Pressure**: Coding under time constraints can be stressful, especially when you're racing against the clock. Timed practice helps you get used to this pressure, so you can handle the stress better during actual tests or competitions.
   - **Mental Toughness**: By regularly practicing under time pressure, you learn to stay calm, avoid panic, and continue thinking clearly even when the time is running out. This emotional regulation is key to performing well in coding tests and interviews.
3. **Improving Speed and Accuracy**:

- o **Faster Problem Solving**: Timed practice helps you identify areas where you need to speed up, whether that's in reading and understanding the problem, writing code, or debugging.
- o **Maintaining Accuracy Under Pressure**: While speed is essential, it's equally important not to sacrifice accuracy. Timed practice helps you learn how to balance both. Over time, you'll be able to solve problems faster without compromising on correctness.

How to Prepare Using Timed Practice

Timed practice is best approached gradually, starting with a focus on understanding the problem and then transitioning into solving it under time constraints. Here's a step-by-step approach:

1. **Start Small**:
   - o **Understand the Problem First**: Initially, solve problems without using a timer. The primary goal is to thoroughly understand the problem, the concepts involved, and how to approach the solution. This builds a foundation and ensures you are solving the problem correctly.
   - o **Concept Mastery**: Once you're comfortable with solving problems without the pressure of time, start practicing with a timer. This helps you simulate real-world conditions where you must not only get the right answer but also do so in a reasonable time frame.
2. **Use Coding Platforms with Timed Challenges**:
   - o **LeetCode**: LeetCode offers timed contests and allows you to practice problems at various difficulty levels, simulating a competitive programming environment. It's an excellent platform to build your skills under time constraints.
   - o **Codeforces**: Known for its regular timed contests, Codeforces lets you practice problems at different difficulty levels. These contests are designed to challenge your problem-solving skills while under time pressure.
   - o **HackerRank, CodeChef, and TopCoder**: These platforms also host timed challenges and competitions, allowing you to practice a wide variety of problems and become accustomed to coding within time constraints. They also provide an excellent community for discussion and problem-solving techniques.

   Tip: These platforms often feature coding contests and challenges, allowing you to test yourself against others and get feedback on how well you're performing under time pressure.

3. **Set Goals**:
   - o **Gradual Time Reduction**: To improve speed, begin by setting yourself reasonable time limits. For example, give yourself 60 minutes for a medium-level problem. As you improve, gradually reduce the time, aiming for 30-40 minutes or less for similar problems. This helps you improve both speed and accuracy progressively.
   - o **Track Improvement**: Monitor how much time you take to solve each problem. Set personal milestones, like completing an easier problem within 15 minutes, and gradually reduce the time for more difficult problems as you get better.

4. **Evaluate Your Performance**:
   - **Post-Solution Review**: After each timed session, review your solution carefully. Reflect on how much time you spent on each phase of the process (problem analysis, algorithm design, coding, and debugging).
   - **Identify Weak Areas**: If you spent too much time on certain sections (like debugging or writing the algorithm), identify why and focus on improving that specific area. For example, if you struggled with algorithm design, study similar problems to get faster at coming up with solutions.
   - **Error Reflection**: If you made mistakes under time pressure, analyze what went wrong. Was it due to rushing through the problem, misunderstanding the question, or making a simple coding error? Use this feedback to refine your problem-solving approach.

- **Limit Time on Each Problem**: For problems that take longer than expected, limit the time you spend on them. This simulates the conditions of a real coding test, where moving on to the next question may be more productive than spending too much time on a single one.
- **Use Timer Tools**: Many coding platforms include timers, but you can also use external tools like a stopwatch or timer apps to track your time. This helps you stay conscious of how much time you're spending on each problem.
- **Take Breaks**: Avoid burnout by taking breaks between timed sessions. After completing a set of problems, take a short break to reset your mind. This helps you maintain focus and performance during each timed challenge.
- **Track Performance Over Time**: As you continue practicing, track your performance in terms of problem-solving speed and accuracy. This gives you a clear idea of your progress and areas for improvement.

---

2. Solving Competitive Programming Problems Using Java

Competitive programming is an excellent way to sharpen your problem-solving skills, boost your algorithmic thinking, and gain proficiency in Java's core features. By solving problems that involve algorithms and data structures, you'll not only become a better coder but also develop the ability to approach complex problems efficiently.

Purpose

Competitive programming problems often require knowledge of advanced data structures and algorithms, and mastering them helps:

- Improve logical thinking and algorithmic problem-solving.

- Get hands-on experience with Java's built-in libraries and core features.
- Hone skills that are essential for technical interviews, coding competitions, and real-world software development.

Key Areas to Focus On

The following are critical areas you should focus on while solving competitive programming problems in Java:

1. Data Structures

Mastering key data structures is critical as they form the foundation for most programming problems. Below are some of the essential ones:

- **Arrays and Strings**:
  - **Basic Manipulations**: Understanding basic operations like finding elements, sorting, and searching is foundational.
  - **Sliding Window Technique**: This helps solve problems where you need to maintain a window of elements (e.g., maximum sum subarray of size k).
  - **Sorting Algorithms**: Understanding bubble sort, quicksort, merge sort, and their time complexities helps in efficiently organizing data.
- **Linked Lists**:
  - Operations like **reversal, merging**, and **detecting cycles** are essential. Linked lists provide a dynamic data structure, which is useful when data size is unpredictable.
- **Stacks and Queues**:
  - These are often used for problems involving **balanced parentheses, expression evaluation**, and **depth-first search (DFS)** in trees.
  - In Java, you can implement stacks and queues using `Stack`, `Queue`, and `Deque` interfaces, or with collections like `LinkedList`.
- **Trees and Graphs**:
  - **Binary Search Trees (BST)**: These trees allow efficient searching, insertion, and deletion operations.
  - **DFS and BFS**: Essential for exploring tree and graph structures. You can implement these using recursion (DFS) or using a queue (BFS).
  - **Graph Algorithms**: Algorithms like **Dijkstra's** (for shortest path in weighted graphs) and **Floyd-Warshall** (for all-pairs shortest path) are vital.
- **Hashing**:
  - Hash maps and hash sets are crucial for problems that require fast lookups. Understanding **hash collisions** and how to handle them is also key.
- **Heaps**:
  - Min-heaps and max-heaps are useful when you need to efficiently get the smallest or largest element in a collection. Java provides a `PriorityQueue` class for this purpose.

Along with data structures, mastering algorithms is a critical component of competitive programming:

- **Sorting and Searching**:
  - o **Binary Search**: Used to find elements or the position of an element in a sorted array.
  - o **Merge Sort, Quick Sort, and Heap Sort**: These are efficient sorting algorithms that help solve problems involving ordered data.
- **Dynamic Programming (DP)**:
  - o DP helps in solving problems where the solution depends on previous subproblems. Common DP problems include:
    - ▪ **Knapsack Problem**: Maximize the value of items you can carry, given a weight limit.
    - ▪ **Longest Common Subsequence**: Find the longest subsequence common to two strings.
    - ▪ **Coin Change Problem**: Find the minimum number of coins needed to make a certain value.
- **Greedy Algorithms**:
  - o These algorithms solve problems by making the locally optimal choice at each step. Problems like **activity selection** and **fractional knapsack** can be solved with greedy approaches.
- **Backtracking**:
  - o Backtracking helps solve problems by exploring all possible solutions and rejecting those that don't meet the criteria. Common backtracking problems include **N-Queens**, **Sudoku solver**, and **permutation generation**.
- **Divide and Conquer**:
  - o Divide and conquer algorithms divide a problem into smaller subproblems and solve them independently. This strategy is used in **merge sort**, **quick sort**, and **binary search**.

Approach for Solving Competitive Problems

When tackling a competitive programming problem, following a structured approach can significantly enhance your chances of solving it efficiently:

1. Understand the Problem:

- **Read Carefully**: Understand the problem statement clearly, paying attention to the constraints and expected output.
- **Break Down the Problem**: Simplify the problem by breaking it into smaller subproblems. Identify what is given and what needs to be computed.

2. Choose the Right Data Structure and Algorithm:

- Based on the problem, choose the most appropriate data structure and algorithm. For instance:

- If the problem involves searching or sorting, an array or binary search tree might be the right choice.
- For problems involving graphs (like finding the shortest path), algorithms like **Dijkstra's** or **Floyd-Warshall** are appropriate.

3. Write Efficient Code:

- **Optimize for Time and Space**: Focus on time and space complexity. For example, if the problem has constraints like large input sizes, consider using an efficient algorithm with lower time complexity, like merge sort over bubble sort.
- **Code Quality**: Ensure the code is clean and understandable, making use of Java's core libraries and best practices (e.g., avoiding redundant calculations and using efficient loops).

4. Code in Java:

- **Use Java Collections**: Java provides powerful collections like `ArrayList`, `HashMap`, `PriorityQueue`, and `HashSet`, which simplify many problems.
- **Custom Classes**: For problems like graphs and trees, where data needs to be represented more complexly, use custom classes to represent nodes, edges, etc.
- **String Handling**: Master Java's `StringBuilder` for efficient string manipulations, as the immutability of `String` objects can be inefficient when concatenating large numbers of strings.

5. Test Your Code:

- After writing your code, test it against:
    - **Sample test cases**: Provided in the problem statement.
    - **Edge cases**: Cases where input might be at extremes (e.g., minimum or maximum input sizes).
    - **Large inputs**: To ensure that your code runs within the time limits for large datasets.

Examples of Java Competitive Programming Problems

Here are a few common types of problems, and how they relate to Java's features:

1. Array Manipulations:

- **Find two numbers that sum up to a target value**: Use a HashMap to store the elements and check for the complement.
- **Merge Sort**: Implement the merge sort algorithm to sort an array in O(n log n) time.
- **Maximum Subarray Sum**: Use Kadane's algorithm to find the maximum subarray sum in O(n) time.

- **DFS and BFS**: Implement depth-first and breadth-first search for traversing graphs or trees.
- **Dijkstra's Algorithm**: Implement this to find the shortest path in a weighted graph using a priority queue.

3. Dynamic Programming Problems:

- **Longest Increasing Subsequence**: Use dynamic programming to find the length of the longest increasing subsequence in an array.
- **0/1 Knapsack Problem**: Use DP to find the maximum value you can carry without exceeding the weight limit.

---

3. Insights for Online Coding Platforms

Online coding platforms are indispensable tools for honing your coding skills, especially for Java coding tests and competitive programming. They offer an extensive collection of problems of varying difficulties and help users learn, practice, and prepare for coding interviews and contests. The platforms come with features like discussion boards, contests, and premium access, providing a structured and comprehensive learning experience.

Popular Online Platforms

1. **LeetCode**

   Overview: LeetCode is a widely popular platform, particularly among developers preparing for coding interviews. It offers a large collection of problems categorized by difficulty, topic, and company-specific questions. LeetCode also allows users to practice coding and participate in coding contests.

   Features:

   - **Problem Sets**: A vast array of problems, ranging from easy to hard difficulty levels.
   - **Contests**: Weekly and monthly coding challenges that help you prepare under timed conditions.
   - **Premium Subscription**: Provides access to exclusive problems and company-specific questions.
   - **Community Discussions**: An active community where users discuss problems, solutions, and optimizations.

Focus Areas:

- o **Data Structures**: Arrays, linked lists, stacks, queues, and trees.
- o **Algorithms**: Sorting, dynamic programming, backtracking, and graph algorithms.
- o **SQL**: Problems that focus on database queries and database-related questions.

---

2. HackerRank

Overview: HackerRank is excellent for beginners to intermediate learners. It offers coding challenges and competitions across a variety of domains, including Java. It's a great platform for those starting with competitive programming or wanting to prepare for job interviews in software development.

Features:

- o **Wide Language Support**: Problems are available in Java and other languages.
- o **Certification**: You can earn certificates after completing coding challenges.
- o **Practice Domains**: You can select specific domains like algorithms, data structures, and artificial intelligence to improve your skills in those areas.

Focus Areas:

- o **Algorithms**: Sorting, searching, and dynamic programming.
- o **Data Structures**: Arrays, stacks, queues, and linked lists.
- o **Artificial Intelligence**: Basic AI concepts, machine learning algorithms, and data science problems.
- o **Databases**: SQL problems for those interested in database management.

---

3. Codeforces

Overview: Codeforces is a popular platform for competitive programming, known for its highly active community and regular contests. It's designed to challenge programmers of all skill levels and is often used by those preparing for international coding competitions.

Features:

- o **Contests**: Offers daily and weekly contests where users can compete under time constraints.
- o **Rating System**: Provides a rating system that ranks users based on their performance in contests, helping you track progress.
- o **Detailed Problem Solutions**: After contests, problem solutions are shared by participants and admins, offering a learning opportunity.

Focus Areas:

- o **Algorithmic Problem Solving**: Emphasis on advanced algorithms like dynamic programming, graph algorithms, and combinatorics.
- o **Time-Complexity Optimization**: Problems that require efficient and optimized solutions under strict time limits.

---

4. **CodeChef**

Overview: CodeChef offers a variety of problems suitable for beginners to advanced learners. It is widely used in competitive programming circles, particularly for preparing for national and international programming contests.

Features:

- o **Contests**: Features long challenges (lasting 10 days) and short contests like Cook-Off and Lunchtime. The long challenges are excellent for tackling more difficult problems.
- o **Problem Sets**: Offers problems from different difficulty levels, with topics spanning algorithms, data structures, and mathematics.
- o **Learning Resources**: CodeChef provides tutorials and learning resources for beginners to improve their skills.

Focus Areas:

- o **Algorithmic Challenges**: Includes sorting, searching, and other algorithm-based problems.
- o **Mathematical Problems**: Problems involving number theory, combinatorics, and discrete mathematics.
- o **Data Structures**: Problems designed to master arrays, linked lists, trees, graphs, and more.

---

5. **TopCoder**

Overview: TopCoder is one of the oldest platforms for competitive programming. It provides algorithmic challenges and timed matches that help build and test your skills.

Features:

- o **Marathon Matches**: These are long-duration challenges that allow you to solve problems in a more relaxed environment.

- o **Single Round Matches**: Time-constrained contests that simulate real-world competitive programming.
- o **Problem Difficulty**: TopCoder challenges are typically more difficult, designed to push participants' limits.

Focus Areas:

- o **Data Structures**: Mastery of arrays, trees, graphs, and hashing.
- o **Algorithms**: Dynamic programming, greedy algorithms, and graph algorithms.
- o **Greedy Algorithms**: Focus on optimization problems that require greedy solutions.

Effective Use of Online Platforms

To maximize your learning experience on these platforms, consider the following strategies:

1. Solve Problems Daily

- Start with easy problems to build confidence and gradually work your way up to medium and hard-level problems. This consistent practice will improve your problem-solving speed and efficiency.
- Set a goal to solve at least one problem every day, dedicating time to both understanding and implementing the solution.

2. Participate in Contests

- Online platforms offer regular coding contests, which are essential for improving your performance under time pressure. These contests help you sharpen both your speed and accuracy, which are key aspects of coding interviews.
- Participating in contests can also provide you with a competitive edge, especially if you aim for top rankings in these contests.

3. Understand Solutions

- If you encounter a difficult problem, don't just look at the solution and move on. Take time to analyze the solution and understand the approach taken.
- Read through community solutions, discuss with peers, and implement these solutions in Java to reinforce your learning. This will also expose you to new techniques and best practices.

4. Review Your Code

- After solving a problem, take time to review and optimize your code. Look for opportunities to improve:
  - o **Readability**: Clean and well-commented code is easier to debug and maintain.
  - o **Efficiency**: Optimize for both time and space complexity, especially if dealing with large datasets.

- o **Edge Case Handling**: Ensure that your code handles edge cases properly, such as extreme input values.

- Most platforms offer leaderboards and progress trackers. Use these features to monitor your growth over time.
- Set milestones and challenge yourself to improve your rankings, whether in terms of solving problems faster or consistently competing in higher-difficulty contests.

Conclusion

Java coding test preparation is a continuous process that involves mastering both core Java concepts and problem-solving skills. Here are the key steps to follow:

- **Practice under timed conditions** to improve speed and accuracy.
- **Solve a wide variety of competitive programming problems** to build a strong foundation in algorithms and data structures.
- **Use online coding platforms** effectively by solving problems, participating in contests, and learning from the community. This approach will help you improve your Java coding skills and succeed in coding tests and interviews.

Types of Replication:

- **Master-Slave Replication**: One node (master) holds the primary copy of the data, and other nodes (slaves) store replicas. Writes are only allowed on the master node, and they are asynchronously propagated to slave nodes. This can introduce delays in synchronization but improves availability.
- **Peer-to-Peer Replication**: Every node in the system is treated equally and can both read and write. This approach improves fault tolerance but can lead to more complex consistency management.

Solution for Replication:

- **Quorum-Based Replication**: This involves reading and writing data from a quorum of replicas. This helps to strike a balance between consistency, availability, and performance.
- **Eventual Consistency**: This is a model where, over time, all replicas will converge to the same state, but temporary inconsistencies are allowed. This is particularly useful in systems where availability is prioritized over strict consistency.

4. Advanced Eviction Policies

Eviction policies are used to determine which data should be removed from the cache when it becomes full. While **LRU (Least Recently Used)** is one of the most common policies, there are several other advanced eviction strategies that may better suit specific use cases.

Types of Eviction Policies:

- **LRU (Least Recently Used)**: The cache evicts the least recently accessed item. It assumes that the least recently used items are less likely to be used in the future. While simple, LRU may not be the best choice for applications where some data needs to be accessed more frequently than others (e.g., popular items).
- **LFU (Least Frequently Used)**: In LFU, the cache evicts the item that has been used the least frequently. This approach ensures that frequently used data remains in the cache, which can be beneficial when some items are more important than others.

    Example: If data item "A" is accessed 10 times and data item "B" is accessed 5 times, under LFU, "B" would be evicted if space is needed.

- **TTL (Time-to-Live)**: In this policy, items in the cache have an expiration time, after which they are considered stale and removed. This is useful for caching data that changes over time and is not needed indefinitely (e.g., session data, temporary results).

    Example: A cached item might have a TTL of 10 minutes. After 10 minutes, the data will be evicted regardless of its access frequency.

- **Random Eviction**: This policy removes a random item from the cache when it is full. It is not as efficient as LRU or LFU but can be used in scenarios where no clear eviction strategy is required.

Choosing the Right Eviction Policy:

The choice of eviction policy depends on the application's access patterns:

- **LRU** works well for most use cases, especially when access patterns are unpredictable.
- **LFU** is suitable when certain items are used more frequently than others and need to stay in the cache longer.
- **TTL** is helpful when the data has a limited lifespan or can become stale over time.

These types of mock interview problems and solutions help candidates prepare for real-world coding challenges in interviews. They emphasize critical problem-solving skills, debugging expertise, and the ability to design scalable systems.

CHAPTER-4

Best Practices and Tips for Success

In competitive programming and Java development, achieving success isn't just about solving problems; it's also about writing efficient, maintainable, and scalable code. Understanding the internals of the Java Virtual Machine (JVM) can further boost performance and optimize resource usage. Below are two key areas that will significantly enhance your coding skills: **Writing Readable and Maintainable Code** and **Understanding JVM Internals for Performance Optimization**.

Writing Readable and Maintainable Code

In any programming environment, writing clean, understandable, and maintainable code is essential for long-term success. Code that is readable and easy to maintain helps developers troubleshoot, enhance, and scale applications without creating unnecessary complexity. Here are some best practices to follow to ensure your code is readable and maintainable:

---

a. Consistent Naming Conventions

Naming conventions in programming are rules for naming variables, methods, classes, and other entities. Consistent naming improves readability and understanding of the code.

Variable Names

- **Descriptive Names**: Always use descriptive names that convey the purpose of the variable. For example:
    - **Good**: `totalSalary, userAge, totalPrice`
    - **Bad**: `ts, a, b`
- **Avoid Single-letter Variables**: Single-letter variable names should be avoided except in very short and simple contexts (like loop counters). For example:
    - **Loop Counter Example**: `for (int i = 0; i < n; i++)`
    - **Bad**: `int a = 5; int b = 10;`

Method Names

- **Use Verbs**: Since methods perform actions, their names should reflect that. For example:
    - **Good**: `calculateTotalSalary(), sortArray(), findUser()`
    - **Bad**: `salary(), array(), user()`

Class Names

- **Use Nouns**: Classes represent objects or concepts, so they should be named using nouns that clearly indicate their role. For example:

- o **Good**: `Employee, BankAccount, Order`
- o **Bad**: `DoSomething, Handler, Processor`
- **Follow Capitalization Standards**: Class names should be written in Pascal case (first letter capitalized), such as `EmployeeDetails`, **not** `employeeDetails`.

Constants

- **Uppercase with Underscores**: Constants in Java should be named in uppercase, with words separated by underscores. For example:
  - o **Good**: `MAX_SIZE, PI, DEFAULT_TIMEOUT`
  - o **Bad**: `MaxSize, pi, DefaultTimeout`

---

b. Commenting and Documentation

Comments help explain the purpose and functionality of the code, making it easier for others (and yourself) to understand it later.

Commenting Code

- **Explain Why, Not What**: Always explain why the code does something, especially when the logic is complex or not immediately clear. For example:
  - o **Good**: `// Check if user is logged in before displaying sensitive data`
  - o **Bad**: `// Initialize the user object`
- **Use Comments for Complex Logic**: If a piece of logic is complex, leave a comment explaining its purpose. For example:

```
// Iterate over all active users and calculate total active time
for (User user : activeUsers) {
    totalTime += user.getActiveTime();
}
```

Javadoc Comments

- **Use Javadoc for API Documentation**: Java provides the Javadoc tool for generating documentation from comments. Every public class and method should be documented with Javadoc comments to improve code maintainability and facilitate automatic documentation generation.

```
/**
 * This method calculates the total salary of an employee.
 * @param basicSalary the base salary of the employee
 * @param bonus the bonus earned by the employee
 * @return total salary after adding bonus
 */
public double calculateTotalSalary(double basicSalary, double bonus) {
    return basicSalary + bonus;
}
```

- **Avoid Commenting Obvious Code**: Do not comment on simple statements or code that is self-explanatory. For example:

```
int x = 5;  // Initializing x to 5 (no need to comment here)
```

- **Focus on Explaining Non-Obvious Logic**: Comments should be used to explain why a piece of code exists or why a certain approach was chosen.

---

c. Code Formatting and Indentation

Consistent formatting is key to making code readable and easy to follow.

Indentation

- **Consistency is Key**: Use consistent indentation throughout your code. The most common style is 4 spaces or a tab. This helps maintain the structure and readability.
- **Example**:

```
if (x > 0) {
    System.out.println("Positive");
} else {
    System.out.println("Non-positive");
}
```

Line Breaks and Logical Blocks

- **Separate Logical Blocks**: Use line breaks to separate distinct logical sections of your code, such as method definitions, loops, and conditional statements.
- **Example**:

```
public void processOrder(Order order) {
    // Validate order
    if (!isValid(order)) {
        return;
    }

    // Process payment
    processPayment(order);
}
```

Using IDE Tools

- **Automatic Formatting**: Use tools built into your IDE (like IntelliJ IDEA, Eclipse, or Visual Studio Code) to format your code automatically according to the Java coding standards.

---

d. Use Functions to Avoid Repetition (DRY Principle)

The **DRY (Don't Repeat Yourself)** principle encourages the reuse of code to avoid duplication and reduce errors.

Avoid Code Duplication

- If you find yourself repeating the same code multiple times, consider creating a function that can be reused.
- **Example**: Instead of repeating the same logic in multiple places:

```java
public void printCustomerDetails(Customer customer) {
    System.out.println("Name: " + customer.getName());
    System.out.println("Email: " + customer.getEmail());
}
```

- **Refactor Repeated Code into Functions**: If the logic is common across multiple parts of your codebase, refactor it into a reusable function. This not only avoids duplication but also makes maintenance easier when the logic needs to change.

---

e. Error Handling and Exception Management

Proper error handling is crucial for writing robust, maintainable, and user-friendly code.

Use Try-Catch Blocks

- **Handle Exceptions Appropriately**: Wrap potentially error-prone code in `try-catch` blocks to catch and handle exceptions.
    - **Avoid Empty Catch Blocks**: Never leave `catch` blocks empty. Log or handle exceptions in a meaningful way to make debugging easier.

```java
try {
    int result = 10 / 0;
} catch (ArithmeticException e) {
    System.out.println("Error: " + e.getMessage());  // Log the error
}
```

Custom Exceptions

- For domain-specific issues, consider creating custom exceptions that can provide more clarity about the error.

```java
public class InsufficientFundsException extends Exception {
    public InsufficientFundsException(String message) {
        super(message);
    }
}
```

f. Following Design Patterns and Best Practices

Design patterns are proven solutions to common problems that can improve the scalability and maintainability of your code.

Use Design Patterns

- **Singleton Pattern**: Ensures that a class has only one instance and provides a global point of access to it.
- **Factory Pattern**: Provides a way to create objects without specifying the exact class of the object that will be created.
- **Strategy Pattern**: Defines a family of algorithms and allows them to be interchangeable.

These patterns can help structure code in a way that is easy to extend and maintain.

SOLID Principles

- **Single Responsibility Principle (SRP)**: Each class should have only one reason to change, meaning it should only have one job or responsibility.
- **Open/Closed Principle (OCP)**: Software entities should be open for extension but closed for modification. This encourages creating classes that can be extended without changing their existing code.
- **Liskov Substitution Principle (LSP)**: Objects of a superclass should be replaceable with objects of a subclass without affecting the correctness of the program.
- **Interface Segregation Principle (ISP)**: Clients should not be forced to depend on interfaces they do not use.
- **Dependency Inversion Principle (DIP)**: High-level modules should not depend on low-level modules; both should depend on abstractions.

By following the SOLID principles and using design patterns where applicable, you ensure your code remains modular, flexible, and easier to maintain.

3. Understanding JVM Internals for Performance Optimization

The Java Virtual Machine (JVM) is responsible for executing Java bytecode and provides essential services like memory management, garbage collection, and execution of Java programs. Understanding JVM internals can help you optimize your Java application's performance, reduce memory usage, and improve execution efficiency. Let's dive into key components and concepts that contribute to JVM performance optimization.

Understanding the JVM's memory model can significantly improve how your application uses memory, leading to better performance.

1. **Heap:** The heap is where all Java objects are allocated. It is divided into two main regions:
   o **Young Generation:**
      ▪ Contains newly created objects.
      ▪ This area is smaller and more frequently garbage collected.
      ▪ The Young Generation is further divided into:
         ▪ **Eden Space**: Where new objects are initially created.
         ▪ **Survivor Spaces**: Where objects that survive the first round of garbage collection are moved.
      ▪ **Promotion to Old Generation**: Objects that live long enough (survive multiple GC cycles) are promoted to the Old Generation.
   o **Old Generation (Tenured Generation):**
      ▪ This area contains long-lived objects.
      ▪ Garbage collection here is less frequent but more expensive because it involves larger chunks of memory.
      ▪ Objects that live longer are eventually promoted from the Young Generation to the Old Generation.
2. **Stack:**
   o The stack is used for method calls and local variables.
   o Each thread has its own stack, with memory allocated in a **Last-In-First-Out (LIFO)** manner.
   o Local variables, method arguments, and return addresses are stored here.
   o Since the stack is tied to the thread, it's faster and more memory-efficient.
3. **Method Area:**
   o This contains metadata about the loaded classes and methods, including bytecode, static variables, and method information.
   o The method area is shared among all threads, and it's also used for garbage collection of class metadata.
4. **Garbage Collection (GC):**
   o GC is an automatic memory management process that reclaims memory from objects no longer in use.
   o However, improper management of references can lead to memory leaks.
   o The garbage collector's effectiveness can be tuned, and understanding its behavior can prevent unnecessary pauses or slowdowns in your application.

Garbage collection (GC) in Java is a process that automatically manages memory by reclaiming memory occupied by objects that are no longer needed. Understanding the different garbage collectors and optimizing their performance is key to ensuring smooth memory management.

1. **Types of Garbage Collectors:**
   - **Serial GC:**
     - Best for small applications with single-threaded environments.
     - The entire GC process happens in a single thread, which can slow down performance for large applications.
   - **Parallel GC:**
     - Uses multiple threads to perform garbage collection, improving performance for multi-threaded applications.
   - **G1 Garbage Collector (Garbage-First GC):**
     - Designed for large heap sizes and aims to reduce pause times.
     - G1 breaks the heap into regions and performs collection incrementally, focusing on the areas that need the most attention.

2. **Optimizing Garbage Collection:**
   - **Minimize Object Creation:** Avoid creating unnecessary objects that add pressure to the garbage collector. Use object pools or reuse objects where possible.
   - **Avoid Holding Unnecessary References:** Don't hold references to objects that are no longer needed, as this prevents the garbage collector from reclaiming memory.
   - **Memory Profiling:** Use profiling tools like **JVisualVM** or **YourKit** to monitor memory usage and garbage collection cycles. These tools can identify memory leaks or excessive memory allocation.

---

c. JVM Tuning and Performance Optimization

Optimizing JVM settings can significantly improve performance, especially for large applications with high memory and CPU usage.

1. **Heap Size Tuning:**
   - Adjust the initial and maximum heap sizes to control the frequency and duration of garbage collection cycles.
   - Use the JVM flags:
     - `-Xms`: Sets the initial heap size.
     - `-Xmx`: Sets the maximum heap size.
   - **Example:**
     - `java -Xms256m -Xmx2g MyApplication` will start the application with 256MB of memory and allow it to grow up to 2GB.

2. **JVM Flags for Optimization:**
   - JVM offers various flags that can optimize the application's memory and garbage collection behavior:
     - **`-XX:+UseG1GC`**: Enables the G1 garbage collector, which is useful for large heap sizes and low-latency applications.
     - **`-XX:+PrintGCDetails`**: Prints detailed garbage collection logs to analyze and optimize GC performance.

3. **Just-In-Time (JIT) Compiler:**

- o The JIT compiler improves performance by compiling Java bytecode into native machine code during runtime.
- o Use **HotSpot profiling** to identify "hot spots" (frequently executed parts of your code) and optimize them for better performance.

d. Multithreading and Concurrency

Java's support for multithreading can significantly improve performance in applications that need to handle multiple tasks concurrently. Proper thread management and synchronization are essential for optimizing performance.

1. **Thread Pools:**
   - o Instead of manually creating and destroying threads, use the **ExecutorService** framework to manage threads efficiently.
   - o Thread pools allow reuse of threads, reducing the overhead of creating new threads and improving scalability.
2. **Locks and Synchronization:**
   - o **Thread Contention and Deadlocks**: If multiple threads are trying to access the same resource, contention can occur. Careful design is needed to avoid deadlocks, where two threads wait on each other indefinitely.
   - o **Synchronized Blocks**: Use synchronized blocks or methods to prevent multiple threads from accessing critical sections of the code simultaneously.
   - o **ReentrantLock**: A higher-level lock that provides more flexibility and additional features like try-lock and timed lock.

e. Profiling and Monitoring

Regular monitoring and profiling are essential to detect performance bottlenecks, excessive memory usage, and other performance-related issues.

1. **Java Profiling Tools:**
   - o **JVisualVM**: A free profiling tool bundled with the JDK that provides insights into memory usage, CPU consumption, garbage collection, and thread activity.
   - o **JProfiler** and **YourKit**: More advanced profiling tools that offer in-depth analysis and visualization of performance bottlenecks.
2. **Monitoring JVM Performance:**
   - o Regularly monitor JVM performance using tools like **JConsole**, which provides real-time monitoring of memory usage, CPU consumption, and garbage collection activity.
   - o **GC Logs**: By enabling GC logging with the flag -XX:+PrintGCDetails, you can track how often GC occurs and how long it takes. This helps identify inefficiencies or excessive pauses.

Conclusion

Success in Java programming—whether in competitive programming, job interviews, or large-scale applications—relies not just on solving problems but on writing clean, efficient, and maintainable code. Following best practices like consistent naming conventions, good documentation, and error handling ensures that your code is both readable and maintainable.

Understanding JVM internals, such as memory management, garbage collection, and thread management, is essential for performance optimization. By tuning the JVM, profiling your application, and using advanced features like multithreading and just-in-time compilation, you can significantly enhance the efficiency and speed of your Java applications. Combining these practices will lead to more scalable, high-performance, and professional Java code.